THE CROSS-COUNTRY PRIMER

THE *CROSS-COUNTRY* PRIMER

Laurie Gullion

THE LYONS PRESS

To my understanding parents

Printed in the United States of America
10 9 8 7 6 5

Library of Congress Cataloging-in-Publication Data

Gullion, Laurie.
The cross-country primer/Laurie Gullion.
p. cm.
Includes index.
ISBN 1-55821-083-0
1. Cross-country skiing—Handbooks, manuals, etc. I. Title.
GV855.3.G85 1990
796.93'2—dc20 *90-6618*
CIP

Illustrations by Amy Butcher.

Contents

Acknowledgments

The following people inspired and assisted me in developing this skiing primer:

Artist and outdoor educator Amy Butcher whose illustrations reflect her technical understanding and love of skiing.

My unpaid research assistant Bruce Lindwall whose special blend of humor and technical ski knowledge kept me on the right track.

Ken Garber, the unofficial ski librarian at the Northfield Mountain Cross-Country Ski Area, for the use of his personal collection of 10 years of ski articles.

Karhu's Dick Weber for his review of the equipment chapter and his help in trying to keep the information as skier-friendly as possible.

The Nordic and Nordic Downhill examiners from Eastern Professional Ski Instructors of America who have unwittingly contributed the framework for these exercises in the last five years of training sessions.

Preface

I was an Alpine skier in search of new territory when I discovered telemark skiing in Vermont in the early 1980s. Heading away from crowds and into the backcountry began to appeal to me about the time that I discovered a collection of clowns who taught cross-country skiing at the Tucker Hill Ski Touring Center. The association threatened my mental health, but it did wonders for my skiing.

Dick Hall, founder of the North American Telemark Organization (NATO), lead the rediscovery of eastern telemark skiing from Tucker Hill and nearby Mad River Glen, home of the best woods skiing in New England. Dick has an unorthodox and wonderful way of teaching people to ski. I joined one of his earliest telemark clinics because I figured a person who made me laugh so frequently could also liven up a cross-country ski lesson. Skiing skills and comedy, too! An hour into the lesson, the motley crew of students loosened up by skiing up and over a snowbank while Dick gave us Olympic-style points for outrageous landings. A little air time to test the strength of our telemark position upon landing!

Later that season, I stumbled after the Tucker Hill boys on their forays at Mad River Glen and began to see the unlimited possibilities for exploration. Don't look at the trees, they said. Look at the white spaces between them. Don't look at the cliff, they said. Look for a clear white space below it, where you want to land—preferably before the brook. Don't keep your skis rooted to the snow, they said. It's safer to stay in the air.

Thanks, coaches. I learned to leap and jump my way through the Green Mountains and mixed a lot of orienteering with this new sport. In searching for old classic backcountry trails and blazing a few new ones, we skied in the best and worst of weather. White-outs dogged the truly scenic excursions, of course, where I discovered that five feet of visibility doesn't mix well with New England underbrush. One of these days, I'll see the north side of Camel's Hump and the Bolton-to-Trapp's wilderness trail when the sun is out.

When I moved back to Massachusetts, the director of the touring center at Northfield Mountain seemed to think that because I'd been telemark skiing, I could teach track skiing. He never really asked me if I'd actually taught. So I never really admitted that I hadn't. Handed one of those tight little suits and an instructor's manual in the fall, I figured I had plenty of time to study before the season opened.

My mentor was a Tucker Hill boy who went by the alias of Nordic Norm. Norm spoofed the art of ski waxing each year at the Mad River Glen telemark festival, one of the largest in the country, in a comedy skit called "The Last Waxing Show." He took the simplicity right out of skiing and turned it into a science with his crystal-lattice medium transport facilitators (skis), petro-chemical interfaces (waxes), command communicators (bindings), and altitude adjustors (poles). A few study sessions with Norm and I was prepared with the facts. Bring on the beginners!

The Tucker Hill boys and their theatre of the absurd had done me a big favor. Now I could never line up the students and deliver a formal lecture on the physics of skiing. Armed with technical information, I was ready to answer any questions that might arise, but my highest priority was setting the right tone for an enjoyable experience. Maybe even an outrageous one. People learn best when they are loose, relaxed, and willing to risk themselves in a new endeavor. They learn best when they are involved in fun activities, challenged by unusual tasks, in touch with their bodies. I offered activities that involved each individual at his or her own level of ability.

After teaching hundreds of students, I still enjoyed myself with this lighter, active approach. It opened my eyes to new ideas that could meet the needs of everyone in the lesson. It still does.

The activities and exercises in this book are a result of a decade of teaching cross-country skiing. They invite you to experiment with a wide variety of tasks that get you started and then refine your skills. They encourage you to feel how different parts of your body affect your skiing. Above all, they strive to keep you relaxed and ready for more.

—Laurie Gullion

Modern skiing maneuvers are just adaptations of ancient skiing forms. This family scene is from a 16th-century Norwegian woodcut.

The Evolution of Cross-Country Skiing

1

Thousands of years ago people skied across the snowy plains of northern Arctic lands on ten-foot-long skis made from a single piece of wood. Cross-country skiing is the oldest form of the sport of skiing, with roots in the ancient civilizations of Scandinavia. The earliest known record appears on a rock wall on a Norwegian island in petroglyphs dating to 2,000 B.C. The petroglyphs feature the faded image of a person on long, narrow skis about twice the length of the person's height. The harsh climate of Scandinavia and the mountainous regions of the Soviet Union and China, where other remnants of ancients skis have been found, demanded this adaptation to winter travel over deep snow.

Recent references to the growing popularity of "new" techniques in cross-country skiing often overlook its venerable past. The telemark—a low, deep-kneed turn—is skiing's oldest method of turning. The two long, narrow skis formed an even longer arc against the snow when early skiers dropped in a near curtsy and carved extremely stable, gradual turns. The telemark served skiing well for almost four thousand years, before the rise of alpine or "downhill" skiing in this century sent it into obscurity. Its recent rebirth is just a recreation of an ancient technique.

The Norse also discovered the virtues of "skating," lest anyone think this technique is also a new phenomenon in cross-country skiing. As people hunted and fought territorial wars from their skis, they adopted a modified glide-and-skate technique that helped to keep them alive. To ski faster, skiers pushed off with a short skating ski and glided on a long ski. Their primitive forms resembled the marathon skate used by today's skiers.

Skiing as a recreational sport began in the 1800s, when people tinkered with their equipment to improve their performances in local races. They triggered the first major technological improvements. Sondre Nordheim of the Telemark region of Norway, often called the father of modern skiing, modified his leather toe strap by adding a birch heel strap for more control on descents. A new era in skiing was born.

The long length of the original skis, needed for flotation and stability through the slower telemark turn, disappeared with the invention of this first rough binding that increased a skier's control. It allowed shorter skis, which promoted shorter, quicker turns and the use of two shorter poles. Skiers abandoned the one long pole that originally was dragged as an outrigger to slow them and aid in turning.

The military in the European Alps adapted the quicker turns to their steep, mountainous terrain, and Scandinavians introduced the new style to mining towns high in the Rockies and Sierra in this country. Snowshoe Thompson, a Norwegian immigrant, is famous for delivering mail by ski across the passes of the high Sierra—sixty-pound bags carried on twenty-five-pound boards carved from oak. Men like Thompson were a special breed, at home in the mountains, eager for excitement, and interested in the more daring aspects of skiing—racing and ski jumping. Mining companies sponsored racing teams with gold purses for the winners, and each team experimented with a special concoction of "dope" to increase its speed.

As an early ski wax, dope was a combination of an amazing array of ingredients, including balsam of fir, oil of cedar, tar, turpentine, Barbary tallow, and castor oil, to name a few. It was the forerunner of the pine tars still used today on wooden cross-country skis, and the miners' experimentation is similar to what today's manufacturers practice to produce the fastest modern waxes.

Alpine skiing continued to grow in popularity, but the Second World War was responsible for really opening the sport to the general public. When the war forced Americans to prepare for fighting in Europe, the famous Tenth Mountain Division trained men for ski mountaineering and developed a corps of people who would establish the nation's first major alpine ski areas, as well as the National Ski Patrol, when they returned home. The "downhill" industry captured the interest of Americans for almost twenty-five years, before cross-country skiing experienced a renaissance.

The running boom of the 1970s signaled a rising interest in physical fitness, and people looked increasingly to cross-country skiing as a means to stay active in the winter. They also desired inexpensive recreation as well as opportunities to travel away from groomed ski areas and explore the outdoors. Skiers began to rediscover cross-country ski touring in local forests and backcountry skiing in the higher mountains.

Those who ventured into the snowy, little-traveled bowls of the West began to combine the virtues of their alpine equipment with the attributes of Nordic gear. The metal edges and wider alpine boards blended with the free-heeled bindings and softer Nordic boots to give better performance under a wider variety of conditions. They dusted off the telemark turn but also adapted alpine moves like stem christies and parallel turns to the steep descents in these remote areas. Then they returned to the challenge of groomed snow at lift areas and spawned a new generation of "telemark" or cross-country downhill skiers.

Meanwhile, another group of cross-country skiers took to the winding tracks popular in the East and began to compete nationally and internationally in Nordic events. Bill Koch of Vermont won America's first Olympic medal for Nordic skiing in 1976, and the Americans emerged as strong contenders in World Cup races in the 1980s in events long dominated by the Scandinavians. Koch and others began experimenting with new, speedier skating techniques discovered when the wax wore off their track skis in long races.

The first of the "new" skating moves was the marathon skate—one ski in the track and the other angled across the track to get greater push forward, like the old Norse hunters' technique. This half-skate prompted skiers to experiment with a full-skate position where they skied with both skis out of the tracks and pushed strongly off them. Tremendous power and speed characterized the new style, which began to dominate the international race circuit.

Initially controversial (as skiers in other countries scrambled to catch up and learn the moves), skating has become a recognized form of competition known as "freestyle." The beauty of the diagonal stride hasn't been forgotten, however, and the traditional style continues to endure in "classical" races where skating is illegal. Today, recreational skiers have discovered the speed of skating and learned the new moves that help them fly across the snow. Cross-country ski areas have catered to its increasing popularity by grooming trails especially for skating.

These "new" methods in Nordic skiing are really just rediscoveries of old functional techniques that have been greatly refined. They have lead to three popular types of cross-country skiing that we'll explore in this book: classical, freestyle, and cross-country downhill skiing. At the heart of each discipline are basic principles that form the foundation of all skiing, but the equipment and terrain dictate changes that make each discipline unique and challenging.

CLASSICAL SKIING

People often imagine the elegant image of the diagonal stride when they think of cross-country skiing. Arms and legs outstretched, the skier strides across the snow in a graceful, powerful fashion. This traditional move is the most common one in classical skiing, where people ski in groomed tracks or break their own trails through the woods.

Classical skiing is the heart of cross-country skiing because it provides a skier with basic techniques for moving forward. Novices find these traditional techniques to be a reassuring beginning because they offer a stable means to progress from walking on skis to gliding on them.

The track skier uses a variety of moves to handle flat terrain and the hills:

- Diagonal stride
- Uphill diagonal stride
- Herringbone
- Double pole
- Kick double pole

The moves require that skiers use cross-country skis that are waxed or patterned on the base to get good traction. As skiers push off to move forward, the ski grabs the snow momentarily. For that reason, classical moves disrupt continuous glide and are usually slower than skating.

Traditional skiers usually learn the basic moves on light touring equipment because the relatively stable gear eases their introduction to the tracks. Their equipment is also wide enough to allow them to tour local parks and woods where they can create their own tracks.

Other classical skiers refine their technique for "citizen racing," where skiers of all abilities compete on courses of varying lengths, from the common ten-kilometer races to fifty-kilometer marathons. These skiers use lighter, narrower, more responsive equipment that enables them to ski quickly and aggressively in the tracks.

FREESTYLE SKIING

The power and speed of freestyle skiing attracts people who want a new challenge in cross-country skiing. Skiers use various skating maneuvers out of the tracks in a distinctive V-shape formation. Similar to ice skating, the skis glide at an angle across groomed snow rather than straight ahead in the tracks.

Skating requires more effort to learn than does classical skiing because skiers have to glide on one ski at a time. But that doesn't mean skating is beyond the grasp of the beginner skier. Many people are finding that they become better overall skiers because they learned to skate early in their development. The crux of skating is the ability to balance on a gliding ski, and improving this skill leads to better classical skiing, too.

Skiers use these freestyle moves on flat terrain and hills:

Marathon skate	V1
No-pole skating	V2
Diagonal V	V2 Alternate

Skiers glide from ski to ski and push themselves strongly across the snow. They use the edges of their skis to push forward, and because the skis are still gliding while they skate, there is no glitch or lag in the momentum. This continuous gliding makes freestyle faster than classical skiing.

The marathon skate is the only exception to this rule; as a half-skate move in the tracks, it represents the transitional technique between the tracks and pure skating. It's faster than classical moves but not as fast as the other "V" skating maneuvers.

Recreational skiers can skate on their touring equipment, but skiers who enjoy skating usually use equipment designed especially for the sport. The light skis are narrower than touring equipment, are similar to the width that a classical racer chooses, and are designed for the special stresses of skating where the skis are edged repeatedly.

The sport is definitely geared to cross-country ski areas where the packed snow provides good support and allows skiers to move quickly. Skating in new, loose, unpacked snow is a tiring endeavor that gives little pleasure!

CROSS-COUNTRY DOWNHILL SKIING

The challenge of skiing downhill on cross-country skis—in deep powder, icy crust, and hard-packed snow—is an exhilarating one. Free heels test a skier's balance and ability to control the greater speed through the turns. While all cross-country skiers use downhill moves, the sport of cross-country downhill is practiced by skiers on heavier metal-edged skis who handle the same terrain as do their alpine counterparts—and more! Beyond lift areas, these skiers also explore the steep bowls and remote trails of the backcountry.

Familiar as "telemark" skiing, the sport is really a blend of many moves for descending the hills:

- Straight run
- Wedge (snowplow)
- Wedge turn
- Skate turn
- Stem christy
- Parallel turn
- Telemark turn

Mastery of the hills depends upon a person's ability to remain balanced on the skis while handling the speed and steepness of the descent. Learning a variety of downhill moves increases a skier's ability to handle different kinds of terrain, and a telemark skier benefits from learning the turns that traditionally have been viewed as alpine moves.

Although I'll address the cross-country downhill skier in explaining the moves, every skier can benefit from the exercises. Classical and freestyle skiers perform these same turns, though with the knowledge that their skis do not carve through the snow as securely. It often adds to the thrill of descending a steep hill or a narrow trail!

Many cross-country downhill skiers have benefited from the rise of skating in recent years. They found that skating improved their legs' ability to function independently because of its emphasis on one-ski glide. As a result, they returned to their telemark skis more able to steer each ski individually through turns and emerged as more capable skiers.

Children are a prime example of how skiers can easily blend the three styles of skiing and develop strong skills quickly. As an instructor of hundreds of school children each winter, I enjoy their superb mimicking abilities and try to exploit this strength. As skating became a strong part of my skiing, I inadvertently used freestyle maneuvers to ski around in my lessons and watched as the kids would shadow my moves effectively—without specific instruction. They loved skating because it was similar to ice skating and allowed them to move quickly—almost every child's fondest wish! As I experimented with more skating moves in the lesson, I realized that the practice actually improved their classical skiing and downhill moves. Poised on one ski, they became acrobats who not only skied better overall but also hovered on the edge of numerous falls and recovered nicely!

Skiing is skiing, and the foundation skills are the same in each discipline. They strengthen and reinforce strong skiing in each area and enable each person to become an acrobat on skis. The most versatile skier is the person who blends elements of the three disciplines to develop his or her own distinctive style.

Getting Ready

2

Learning how to cross-country ski is easy and enjoyable with the proper equipment. The sport offers a sometimes bewildering array of choices, but skiers can narrow those options to suit the type of skiing that interests them. Determining the nature of your involvement helps you make the best decisions about the most appropriate equipment.

This primer answers basic questions about cross-country equipment to help you understand how the gear affects your skiing. Properly sized equipment that matches snow conditions, terrain, and skiing ability increases enjoyment of the experience. Just ask any skier who has struggled on borrowed skis and poles!

First you need to decide where you will be skiing: in groomed tracks at touring centers, in the backcountry, in citizen's races, on the groomed trails of alpine ski areas. The sport is increasingly specialized with equipment designed for very specific activities and better performance, but you can still choose one set (ski, boots, and poles) that serves a variety of needs without sacrificing a great deal of performance.

While I admit to having perhaps "a few" pairs of skis in the garage to suit a variety of situations, one of my favorites is an old pair of versatile touring skis. They allow me to head out the back door in fresh snow, skim along the local snowmobile route, and veer off into the woods to create my own trails. Having the ability to experience a variety of conditions on one pair of skis shouldn't be overlooked in these days of specialization.

To help you choose, this section addresses the generic characteristics of three major types of equipment: classical, freestyle, and cross-country downhill.

Classical

Light touring equipment is the most popular because of its multipurpose use. These skis can be used in and out of tracks where their medium width "floats" or supports you in unpacked snow. Racing skis are lighter and designed primarily for higher-performance track skiing. Their narrower width eliminates drag in the tracks and increases gliding speed. Skiers often choose these more responsive skis as their skiing improves.

Freestyle

Skating equipment is designed for groomed snow where skiers get good traction by edging their skis in a V-shaped position. Reinforced sidewalls on the skis withstand the stresses of skating. These skis are available in a wider width that gives novice skaters increased stability and a narrower width for the more experienced who want faster glide. Although classical skis can also be used to skate, they may not have been constructed originally to be set on edge repeatedly. Skaters also use longer poles to keep them behind the wider V-position of the skis.

Cross-Country Downhill

Telemark equipment resembles alpine more than Nordic gear. Appropriate for high-speed downhill skiing or the unpacked snow of the backcountry, the skis are wider, with metal edges, and require a heavier boot-and-binding system. Shorter alpine poles let skiers plant them upright for turning. Lighter gear is appropriate for general touring, but as skiers desire greater speed and more radical terrain, the equipment must be heavier and more durable for greater skiing control.

SKI SELECTION

Modern manufacturing has greatly changed the materials from which skis are made. Laminated wood skis have given way to synthetic materials like fiberglass, foam, and polyurethane that improve a ski's performance and durability.

The first decision is whether the skier wants a waxable or nonwaxable ("no-wax") ski. With a *waxable* ski, the skier applies a thin layer of wax to the base of the ski to suit the day's snow. A major benefit is that the skier can adjust the wax as needed to suit a wide variety of conditions. He or she can fine-tune the wax for increased glide and/or grip (traction). Waxable skis are appropriate for the three disciplines and offer better performance.

The *nonwaxable* ski has a pattern molded into the underside that provides traction. Convenience is a major reason no-wax skis are enormously popular with recreational skiers. They are best suited for climates with warmer, wet snow, but they do not glide as well as a properly waxed ski does. A nonwaxable ski is difficult for skating and classical racing because the pattern grabs the snow and slows the ski. Telemark skiers at lift areas avoid no-wax skis because of the terrain's higher speeds, which can destroy the patterned base. No-wax skis are very appropriate for light touring and backcountry touring, especially where snow conditions may vary and make waxing difficult.

Beyond the basic types of skis, these characteristics also affect a skier's choice: camber, length, width, and flex.

Camber

The arc or bow in the center of a ski is its *camber,* and all skis have some camber. The amount of force needed to stand on one ski and flatten it against the snow affects how the ski handles. A ski with stiff camber needs more force to flatten the bow. A ski with soft camber

Camber refers to the bend in the middle of a ski where the wax pocket is located.

needs little or no force; your weight may be enough to depress the ski.

The camber affects how a ski slides across the snow. On a light touring ski, a *wax pocket* exists in the midsection of the ski, under your foot. A ski needs enough camber to lift the wax pocket off the snow when you glide with your feet side by side. Here the camber lets you ski easily on the tips and tails of the ski without the wax pocket dragging on the snow and slowing the skis. But when you stand on one ski and press the wax pocket into the snow, the camber allows the ski to grip the snow so you can gain the purchase to move forward.

A telemark ski designed for skiing at a lift area has a softer "alpine" camber. The ski can be pressed against the snow easily and uniformly to carve turns. Within this "soft" range, a stiffer camber is better for hard, icy conditions, and a softer camber is better for loose, powdery conditions.

Many skiers use the same telemark ski for groomed alpine areas and backcountry skiing. They simply apply grip wax in the midsection or "climbing skins" to scale the hills. But some telemark skis are designed with a nonwaxable base primarily for backcountry use. They tend to have more camber, similar to a light touring ski, to handle undulating terrain.

A person's weight affects the degree of camber needed in a ski. Heavy, short people usually need a stiffer camber to support their weight. A longer ski also distributes their weight, but they might not be able to handle the increased length. Selecting too stiff a camber for your weight prevents you from flattening the ski to get good traction. Light people need a softer camber.

Skiing ability also affects the camber. Because skilled skiers can press the ski strongly into the snow for grip, stiff camber gives them a more responsive ski with better glide. A novice skier is usually happier with a softer camber that takes less force to use properly.

Length

Proper ski length is affected by the skier's height, weight, and skiing ability. A light skier may choose a slightly shorter ski, while a heavy skier may opt for a longer ski. Novice skiers may find a shorter ski is easier to handle and steer at first, but they'll eventually welcome the stability and increased speed of a longer ski.

These general rules apply for choosing the length of a ski:

CLASSICAL The skis reach to the wrist (unless you have unusually long arms!) when you raise an arm above your head. Another guide is thirty centimeters over head height for a man and twenty-five centimeters for a woman, assuming that women generally weigh less than men of the same height.

FREESTYLE Skis are approximately ten centimeters shorter than your appropriate classical-ski length, although elite skiers may opt for a longer ski in some snow conditions. (A long ski in loose snow floats better and provides better glide.)

CROSS-COUNTRY DOWNHILL Telemark skis are usually sized by adding twenty-five centimeters to head height, unless you are planning

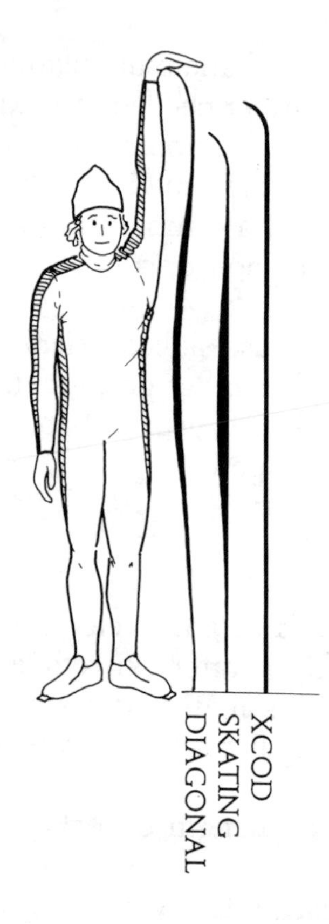

Use these *general* guidelines to select the proper ski length. Length is also affected by the person's weight, ski stiffness and skiing terrain.

to ski primarily in tight, steep places. Then, adding twenty centimeters is a good rule.

Width

Skis vary in their width from tip to tail, and their shape determines how the ski performs under different snow conditions. Width affects the support the skis offer in loose snow, the ski's speed in the tracks, and the ski's ease of turning. A wider ski offers better support (more flotation), and a narrower ski provides more speed (less resistance to the snow).

The narrowest skis are approximately forty-four centimeters wide at the "waist" (middle) and are usually designed for classical and freestyle racing. Light touring skis range up to fifty centimeters, with the wider end more appropriate for out-of-track skiing. Cross-country downhill skis usually approximate fifty-five centimeters or greater at the waist.

The difference in width measurements along the ski's length is called *sidecut,* and it refers to the degree to which a ski is shaped like an hourglass. A ski has sidecut when it is wider at the tip and tail and narrower at the waist. Sidecut makes the ski easier to turn. When a ski is edged, the camber is reversed into an arc. The entire edge of the ski carves through the snow and follows the arc to turn the ski.

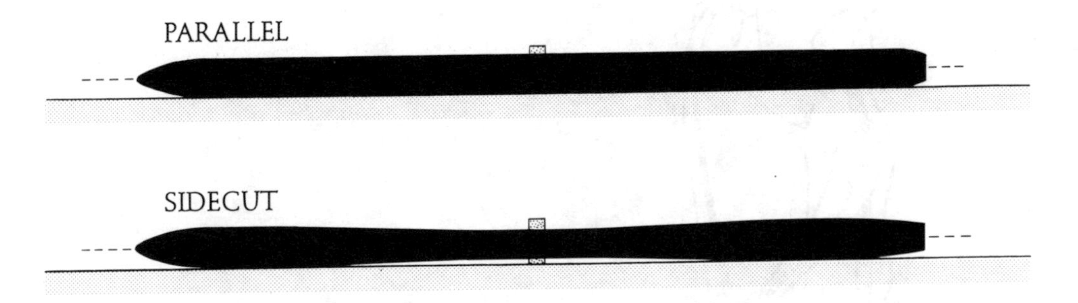

A ski with a *parallel* cut has the same width at the tip, waist, and tail. It tracks in a straighter line. A ski with *sidecut* is narrower at the waist than the tip and tail. It turns more easily.

Cross-country downhill skis have sidecut to increase their turning ability, but the degree of sidecut will vary a great deal. The greater the tip width, the quicker the turning. Track and skate racing skis have a *parallel cut* (more equal measurements at the tip, waist, and tail), or *negative sidecut* (narrower tip or tail than waist). These measurements improve the ski's tracking and limit turning.

Flex

A ski's flexibility is measured in two ways: along its length and torsionally (around a central axis). How well the ski performs is a function of the two types of flex and their interrelationship.

An even flex along the whole length is important to cross-country downhill skiers who want the ski to form a smooth arc from tip to tail when turning. The ski will turn easier than will a stiff-cambered racing ski whose camber interrupts the even flex. Flex can also vary in the tip and tail, and you test it by placing the tail on the ground and pulling the tip toward you or pushing away against the tail.

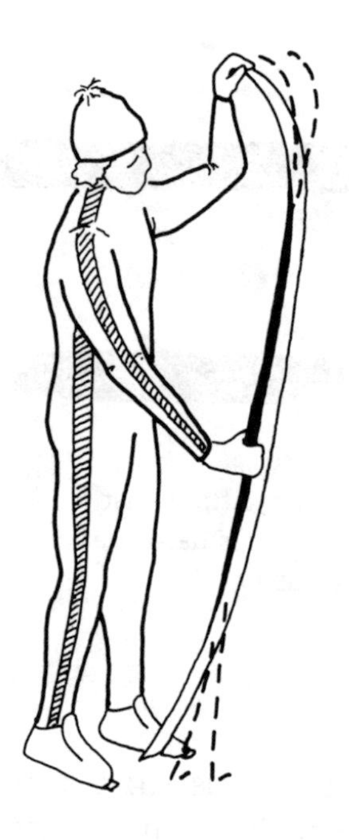

The *flex* or stiffness of a ski can be tested by pulling and pushing on the tip and tail.

A soft flex in the tip allows a ski to ride over and absorb changes in terrain. Classical racing skis have a soft tip that follows the tracks without climbing out of them. But the flex tends to extend only a short way down the ski. A tip that flexes farther down, nearer the waist, is suitable for touring in the backcountry in loose snow and provides better flotation and turning. A stiff tip holds hard-packed snow better and is found in telemark skis used at alpine ski areas.

Tail flex is similar to tip flex in its effects. A short tail rides easily over terrain, but it may wash out during a turn if it is too soft. Most skis have a slighter stiffer tail than tip and offer the skier added support.

Torsional flexibility or rigidity is the last element that affects the ski's performance, and you test it by twisting the tip of the ski. Some torsional flexibility is desired in track skis for shock absorption and the ability to stay in the tracks around corners. A more torsionally rigid tip in a telemark ski holds a better edge under icy conditions. The skating ski has high torsional rigidity to hold an edge against the snow and provide a proper platform from which to move the other ski.

The Right Skis

Ski manufacturers eliminate the guesswork and provide general guidelines that match a skier's weight to the length and flex of a ski. These charts usually distinguish between recreational and elite skiers in their ratings and offer a good guide in ski selection.

The best testing occurs on snow, and there is no substitute for renting or borrowing skis before buying. Many skiers also field-test higher performance skis that are available from better ski shops and at manufacturers' demonstration clinics. You can get a real feel for how the skis perform for you and a much better sense of what is appropriate for your weight and skiing ability.

A simple "paper" test for classical skis can also provide some insight into whether these skis are right for you. This test determines if the camber is appropriate for your weight. Wear the skis indoors on a hard surface and position your feet side by side as if you are sliding downhill. The skis should rest on their tips and tails, allowing a piece of paper to be slid under the midsection. If the paper doesn't fit, the skis are too soft. If the paper slides in front of the feet about six inches and slightly behind the heels, then the camber is right. This area is the wax zone on a waxable ski.

The second part of the test is to stand completely on one ski with the paper under the foot. If the paper can't be moved, it shows that you can depress the camber and get good grip against the snow. If the paper moves, the ski is too stiff and you are unable to depress it enough.

BOOTS AND BINDINGS

In recent years technology has created many very good boot-and-binding systems beyond the traditional seventy-five-millimeter "three-pin" system. Many manufacturers produce a boot-binding combination unique to their company that may not be interchangeable with another ski system. The best approach is to find a *comfortable,* stable boot designed for your style of skiing. Selecting a specific boot usually dictates the choice of a matching binding.

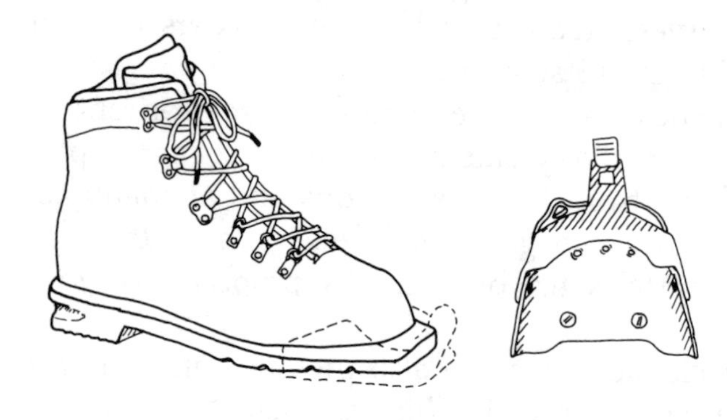

This heavier *three-pin* boot-and-binding system is used for cross country downhill skiing.

The best all-around telemark boot is a heavy leather one with an above-the-ankle cut. But some select taller shin-height models with more plastic reinforcement for higher performance; these boots offer greater support on race courses and radical terrain. Many telemark skiers use the simple seventy-five-millimeter binding, but it's a durable aluminum-alloy version of the touring model that affords good control on downhills. Some choose cable bindings for even greater control, or the new releasable bindings for improved safety at high speeds.

Light touring boots have changed dramatically from the old seventy-five-millimeter system to offer skiers more comfort and better performance. The old system bound the boot to the ski at the toes and the boot flexed with each step. The new systems use a binding that flexes, rather than the boot, to enhance comfort. The boot construction also offers more lateral or side-to-side stability to improve balance and turning. The boots come in below- and above-the-ankle cuts.

Lateral stability becomes very important in skating boots, where skiers are setting their skis on edge. Skating boots usually have reinforced side construction with an above-the-ankle cut.

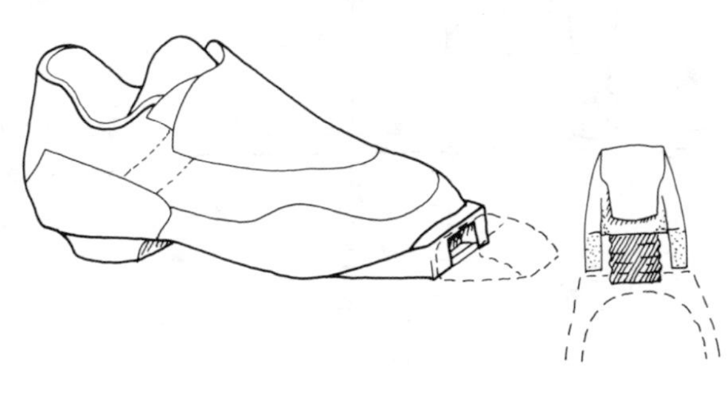

Classical skiers can use a low-cut light touring boot and binding.

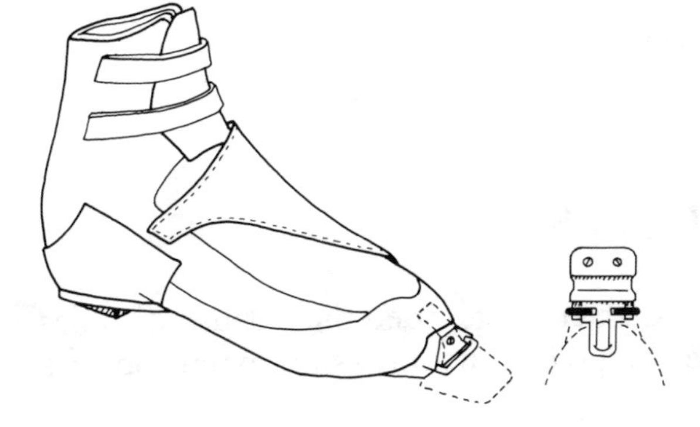

Freestyle skiers can use a reinforced boot for greater lateral stability while skating.

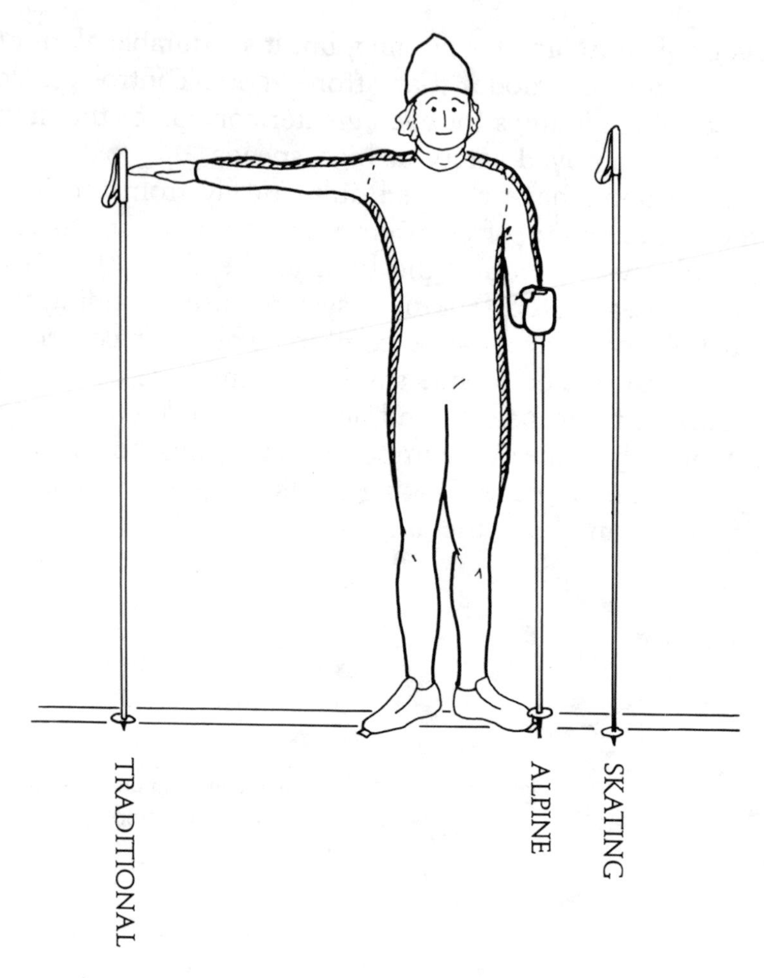

Select the proper pole length with these general guidelines.

POLES

Although power stems from the skier's legs, the efficient use of poles greatly enhances skiing. Because the poles function as an extension of a skier's arms, ski-pole length is an important consideration. Skiers select poles that fit their size and intended use.

Traditional skiers now use a longer pole that reaches to shoulder height. This added length (the original measurement was to the underarm) keeps the poles in an angled position and increases the extent of the poling phase. A pole that is substantially shorter ends up in a vertical position that gives the skier less forward push.

Freestyle skiers follow the "moustache rule" in selecting poles that reach to a point between their mouth and nose. The additional length helps to keep the poles behind the body and V-position of the skis. It also increases the poling power and complements the speedier nature of skating—a faster style than traditional diagonal-stride skiing.

Telemark skiers who ski at lift areas choose a shorter aluminum alpine pole because the pole is planted more upright. The pole-plant functions more as a timing device and serves less as a power booster. The proper length is gauged by turning the pole upside down and grabbing just below the basket. Your arm should form a right angle at the elbow.

Skiers in the backcountry often choose a pole with a height halfway between an alpine and a traditional cross-country pole. This compromise gives them a pole long enough to provide some pushing power on the flats but short enough to plant on the downhills. Another option is adjustable poles that tighten or loosen by twisting an internal mechanism that locks them at the desired height.

Recreational skiers apply less stress to their poles, and basic fiberglass poles are sufficient for them. Racers, especially skaters, need a stiffer, stronger reinforced pole that stands up to the increased stress. A wide range of poles are available in both recreational and performance models.

Proper pole grip can enhance your performance. Wear the pole strap like a bracelet and grab the pole *above* the strap. When the strap on a cross-country pole is adjusted properly, the top of the grip rests in the web of the hand (between the thumb and forefinger) when the pole is extended behind the body. This tightness allows you to relax the hand after poling but to recover the pole quickly to bring it forward.

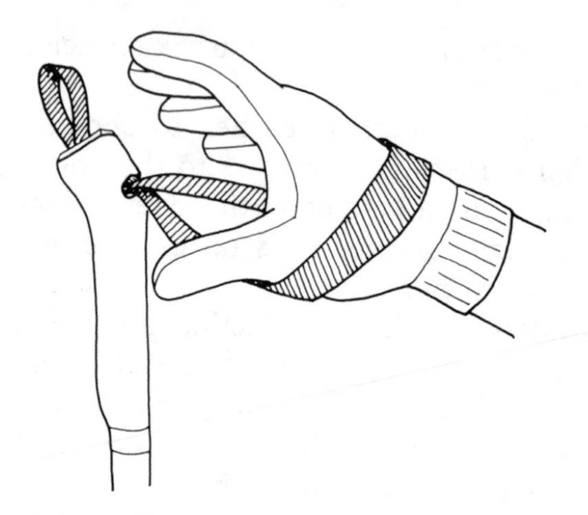

The hand comes up through the webbing before grabbing the pole for good grip.

WAXING

Wax provides skiers with momentum, and it allows them either to grip the snow or glide on it. *Grip* occurs when the ski adheres momentarily to the snow to provide traction, and the skier pushes off to move forward. *Glide* happens when skis slide with little resistance from the snow or ski.

Skiers wax traditional skis for optimum grip and glide; they have a grip zone in the midsection and glide zones at the tip and tail. The grip wax in the midsection provides a cushion to which the snow sticks for good traction. The wax is just sticky enough for the snow crystals to adhere when a skier steps on the ski. But the wax must also release the snow crystals when the ski is lifted and the skier moves forward.

The glide wax on the tip and tail smooths the surface and reduces friction to increase speed. Skiers wax the entire length of skating and telemark skis for glide alone.

Experienced skiers enjoy the experimentation that waxing invites, and some raise it to an art form! Picking the right wax is an educated guess for even the best racers. Novice skiers find that a few simple principles can make the process an uncomplicated one. Let's explore the relationship between the wax and snow.

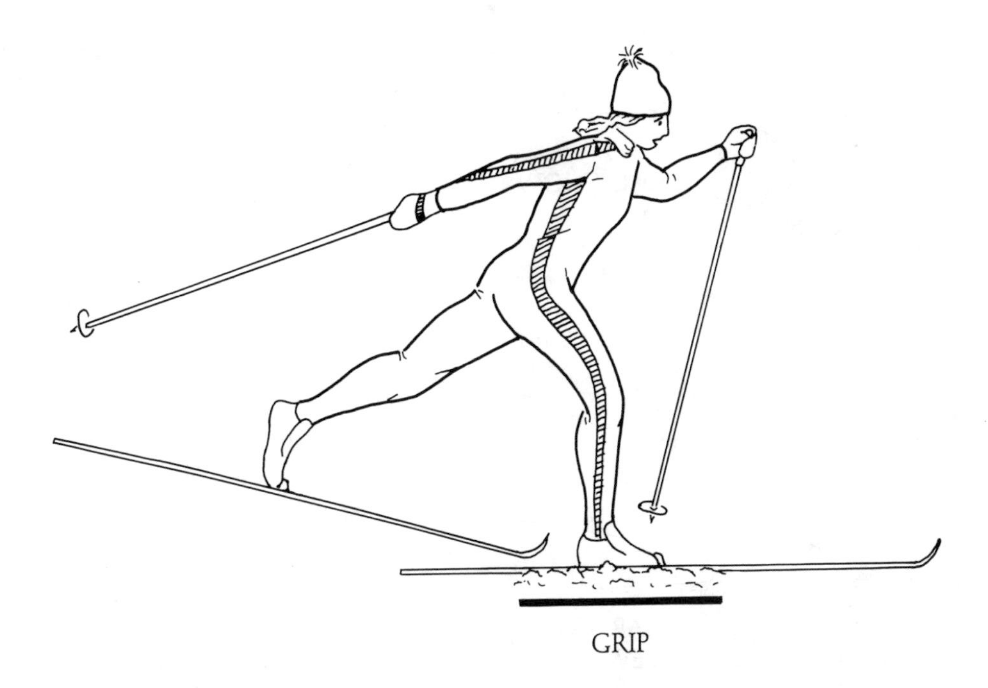

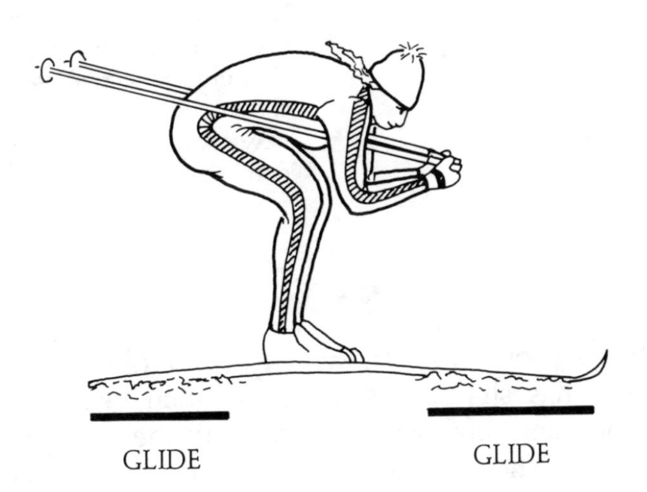

A skier presses the wax pocket into the snow and gets good grip or traction to move forward. Sliding on two skis distributes the weight over both skis and lets the skier glide on the tips and tails.

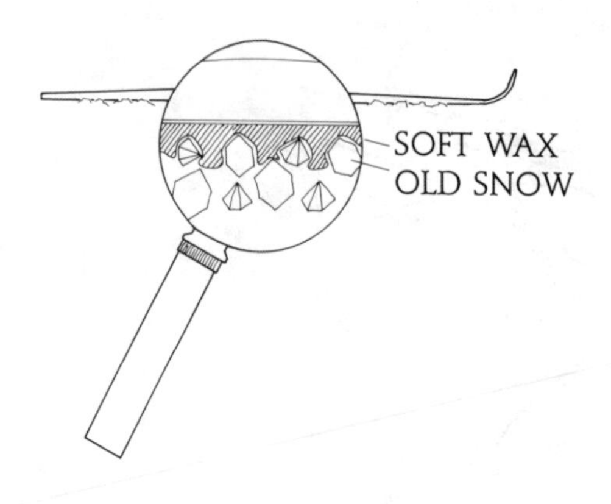

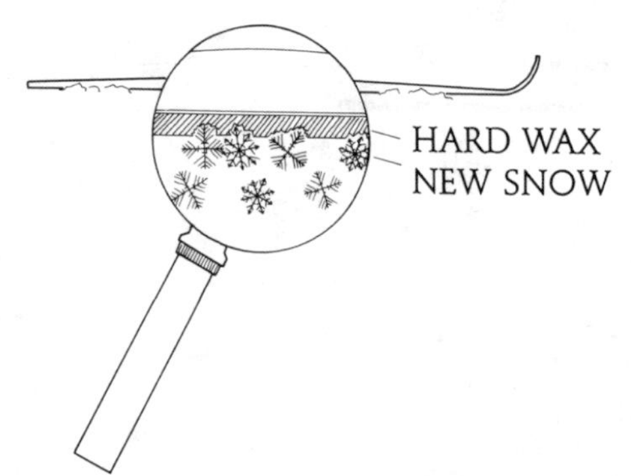

Understanding the relationship between the snow and the wax is helpful for effective waxing. Old snow requires a softer wax, while new snow needs a harder wax for good traction.

Snow

Weather affects snow crystals, which are highly unstable in nature. Fresh cold snow has sharp, jagged edges much like carpet tacks. But warmer days melt and refreeze the snow, and these jagged points begin to soften over time. The crystals become rounded and function more like ball bearings.

To achieve an effective bond between the snow and wax, an inverse relationship exists. New, abrasive snow needs a hard, smooth wax to prevent the jagged crystals from penetrating too deeply. Old, rounded snow needs a soft, tacky wax that grabs the crystals.

Grip and Glide Waxes

Two types of grip waxes exist: *hard* wax for cold temperatures and newer snow, generally for several days after a new snowfall, and *soft* wax or *klister* for warmer temperatures and refrozen snow or icy tracks. Hard waxes come in small tins for easy application, and klisters look and function like toothpaste. All waxes are color-coded to show their range from cold/new to warm/old snow conditions.

For skiers who want to simplify waxing, the easiest approach is the "two-wax" system for "dry" (new) conditions and "wet" (old) conditions. When temperatures reach above freezing, the wet wax works best. Below freezing, choose the dry wax. This convenient system gets people skiing without fuss and works reasonably well.

Glide waxes are also made in different hardnesses and follow the same principles as above. New/cold snow needs the hardest glide waxes, and old/wet snow needs the softest. Designed to enhance glide, these waxes are also tailored to alpine and Nordic skiing. Telemark skiers at lift areas use a more durable glide wax that handles the increased friction of high speeds.

Wax Application

Skiers rub grip waxes on the midsection as they would use crayons in a coloring book. Then they smooth out the application by rubbing the wax with a cork. The rubbing generates friction and bonds the wax to the ski base.

Klisters ooze from a tube similar to a toothpaste tube, and must be squeezed carefully onto the midsection. Only a thin application is necessary. Klisters spread easily with an applicator and cover the base to either side of the groove. Best applied indoors in the warmth, these soft waxes need to harden outdoors before skiers place the skis on the snow. Otherwise, the snow crystals stick to the wax.

Skiers usually melt glide waxes onto the ski and "iron" it in with a waxing iron to get a deeper penetrating bond. They scrape the excess wax from the ski to leave a thin layer on the base and also remove any wax from the central groove to allow the ski to track.

A ski needs glide wax when the base begins to show a slight whiteness, a telltale sign of dryness. Skating skis tend to wear more heavily on the inside edge, where the whiteness can first appear. Waxing the no-wax ski helps it to glide better and preserve the base. Glide-wax only the tips and tails, however, because any wax applied to the patterned midsection interferes with good traction.

CLOTHING

Cross-country skiing is an energetic sport where skiers burn five hundred to seven hundred calories an hour if they are moving at a speed of five miles per hour. Most novices find they have overdressed for the activity and need to shed clothing to be comfortable. Warmer clothing is needed by telemark skiers riding lifts at alpine areas.

Every skier benefits by dressing in the layering system common to participants in every cold-weather sport. Layering helps people regulate their body temperatures so their energy is directed toward the activity rather than toward staying warm or cool. Three layers are important.

WEATHER PROTECTION. The outer layer protects you from weather changes like wind or rain and is usually waterproof or windproof. It provides a shield against the weather and can be removed easily. Parkas are perfect for telemark skiers but too warm for traditional or freestyle skiers unless they want a sauna under their clothes.

INSULATION. This middle layer provides warmth. Sweaters and syn-

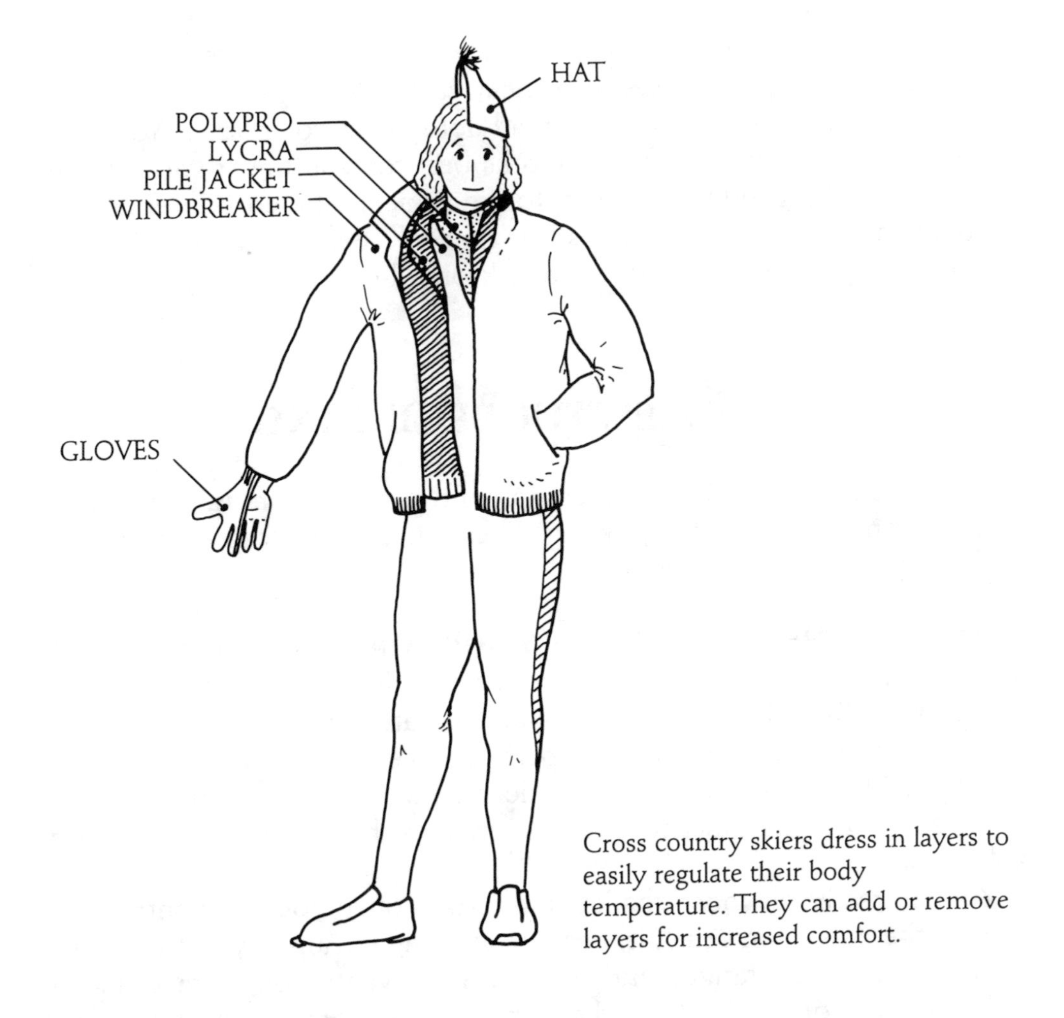

Cross country skiers dress in layers to easily regulate their body temperature. They can add or remove layers for increased comfort.

thetic pullovers are best, especially if they are light and can be packed away easily. Even this layer can be too much for strenuous touring.

WICKING. The layer closest to the skin needs to move perspiration away from the body, where it chills you, into outer layers. Synthetic and natural-fiber long underwear does this well as long as the material is not cotton. Cotton remains cold when wet and becomes chilling even during a short break from skiing. People who ski actively often wear one-piece lycra suits that help them ventilate heat easily.

What one person defines as cold may not be cold to another. You must discover the layering system that works best for you under various conditions. There's a good reason why touring skiers who encounter numerous uphill and downhill situations bring a pack! Be knowledgeable about your clothing needs before you embark on all-day tours.

A SUCCESSFUL BEGINNING

Beyond choosing appropriate equipment, other factors influence your introduction to cross-country skiing. These suggestions can help to make your early experiences successful.

1. MATCH THE TERRAIN TO YOUR ABILITIES. Flat or gentle terrain is a good place to try out the new equipment and develop comfort on skis. Take the time here to warm up and practice basic exercises, because this improves your trail performance. Some skiers may learn quickly with a short warm-up, while others may benefit from several hours spent in a flat practice area that enables them to become comfortable on skis.

You are ready for more challenging terrain once you can control your skis on the flats. Don't rush it, because tackling terrain beyond your abilities causes muscle fatigue and tension. It prevents you from using the right muscles for a task. Be ready to return to gentler terrain when tired; better progress will result.

2. SET REASONABLE GOALS. Because fitness can affect your ability to ski, match the intensity of your practice to your physical abilities. Give yourself enough time to learn to ski (and to make mistakes). Travel shorter distances at the beginning until you discover how far you can ski.

Introduce friends and children to skiing in short sessions and where indoor facilities are accessible. Don't impose your expectations to ski

Begin your practice on gentle terrain where you can develop good skills in a relaxed fashion!

with good style on a child's goal to explore new terrain and ski fast. They care little about final form and usually ski efficiently without thinking about it!

3. KEEP A GOOD PERSPECTIVE. It's better to "ski smart" than foolishly. You can always sidestep down an intimidating hill (or part of the way down until you feel comfortable with the descent). Next time you'll have more confidence to master more, if not all, of the hill. Learn new moves at your own rate; you'll develop more efficient skiing.

Falling is part of the sport—even the best skiers take tumbles! In fact, controlled falling (curling into a ball and sitting down to one side of the skis) is valuable to know and can be used defensively when you build uncontrollable speed.

Remember that skiing is supposed to be fun!

4. PRACTICE BASIC SKILLS FIRST. Practice simple skills before complex moves to establish a solid foundation. Warm up with basic exercises that strengthen fundamental skills. Problems with a maneuver usually stem from a poorly mastered foundation skill. The skills-first approach makes you a relaxed, competent skier who is better able to handle harder challenges. Build on successes!

PERFECT PRACTICE

I watched two friends teach their young sons how to ski, and the dynamic skiing style of these children convinced me that every adult can benefit from their approach. The parents had taught and coached skiing to schools, national teams, and even stars of Hollywood films, and they used a successful approach that blended the teaching of basic skills with the development of a healthy attitude that encourages good skiing.

Their sons grew up in a household where skiing is as normal as walking, and while many adults don't receive this opportunity, all ages can benefit by the same easy step-by-step approach. Concentrating on skill-building enables new skiers to keep their learning clear and uncluttered like the experiences of these children.

At two years, they tromped around the house and backyard on cross-country skis where the rugs and the grass gave them a chance to stand securely and develop good balance. At three years, they slid down gentle, snowy hills and learned to absorb the bumps and dips. By the first grade, they handled difficult downhill and cross-country trails with an awareness of their abilities and, more importantly, their limits.

During the early years, the boys skied for as long or as little as they liked. The parents realized that even twenty minutes could tax their developing muscles, and they wanted them to enjoy the experience. Playing and tumbling in the snow were as important to their comfort and enjoyment as walking and sliding on skis.

There is an important lesson here for all prospective skiers. Making the experience a pleasurable one helps a skier achieve the goal of smooth, fluid skiing more easily. Relaxed, enthusiastic practice tailored to each person's abilities is the best kind of learning. Efficient, enjoyable skiing is every skier's goal, and the next chapter explains how the basic skills provide a foundation for excellent ski technique.

The First Step

3

A group of high school students in a school program played a rousing game of elbow tag, and each skier dashed around the playing field on one ski. To escape being tagged by the person who was "It," two youths skied up to each other and linked elbows to create a "safety zone." After five seconds, they had to ski away again. One teacher watching the intense activity said, "I can't believe how fast they move. And how well!"

These students were beginners, and for many of them the program represented their first day on cross-country skis. I like to use uninhibited games in my ski lessons to strengthen the basic skills important to efficient skiing. The one-ski rule gave these new skiers a chance to control their sliding without a lot of falling. They glided on one ski and turned sharp corners, dodging quickly amongst each other to avoid being tagged. Without knowing they were learning a specific skill in the game, these kids "practiced" intensely and later incorporated their better balance in the "real" moves.

A *skill* is an ability to use the hands or body with dexterity. It is a simple move that usually focuses on one specific task. By contrast, a *maneuver* is more complex because it requires a unique combination of skills to perform a certain function.

Isolating the fundamental skills is an important step for every skier, regardless of age. A complex move is divided into simpler parts for easier practice. By reinforcing the underlying skills first, you have a greater chance of mastering a maneuver like a snow plow or the diagonal stride. Learning skills before maneuvers has proven to be the most effective approach in sports instruction in the past decade.

The activities in this chapter are designed to keep you loose, relaxed, and confident in learning the basic skills. The approach is simple, straightforward, and fun to encourage quick, enjoyable practice. Immerse yourself in this playful approach and use the images to experience the sensation of smooth skiing.

THE EIGHT FUNDAMENTAL SKILLS

The fundamental skills are descriptive and easy to understand, and they help to explain *how* a skiing maneuver happens. Whether one is a beginner or racer, child or adult, a clear picture of skiing emerges. Let's define the skills briefly:

Sliding	Gliding across the snow with a neutral, balanced stance; the feet are side by side.
Gliding on one ski	Balancing on one ski while gliding; the body is centered over the gliding ski.
Moving from ski to ski	Shifting weight from one ski to the other one.

Pushing off	Gripping the snow with the ski to move forward; sometimes known as the "kick" in cross-country skiing.
Poling	Pushing against the poles.
Edging	Digging the bottom corner of the ski into the snow.
Skidding	Slipping the skis sideways across the snow.
Steering	Rotating the foot and leg to turn the ski.

Think of the skills as the building blocks of good technique and combine them in many ways to create different maneuvers. If the foundation isn't strong, your pile of blocks begins to fall down. Striving to perfect the maneuvers without practicing skills can lead to frustration and poor performance.

For instance, skiers use a snowplow to control their speed on downhills. Forget the ultimate goal—the snowplow—at the outset. Isolate each skill first—steering, sliding, and edging—and practice the exercises that strengthen each skill. Then combine them to perform the maneuver. You'll be rewarded when smooth, strong skiing results.

USING THE ACTIVITIES

The best practice is perfect practice. Strive for balanced, coordinated moves rather than bursts of speed or power. John Tidd, a former member of the National Demonstration Team for Professional Ski Instructors of America, says "ski slow to go fast." What he means is that the essence of good skiing is a fluidity that stems from efficient motion. You'll go farther and expend less energy. Consider these points to promote the best practice:

1. VARIETY. Mix up the practice of skills; your muscles appreciate the variety! Exercise legs and arms equally and avoid a dependency on one side of your body. (Many people have a dominant side.)

2. SKIING WITHOUT POLES. Practice many exercises without poles; throwing away these "crutches" at the outset helps to build better balance and good rhythm.

3. DURATION. The activities do not note how many repetitions are recommended because the extent of practice depends upon the individual. You are your best guideline, because your body knows when a move feels secure. The extent of practice can vary between moves, especially if you have one leg that is stronger than the other.

4. INDOOR PRACTICE. Begin right away! Perform the in-place exercises as you read this chapter. Gunde Svan, the Swedish national ski champion, talks about the hours he spends in "television training" each year. Every time he watches television, he strengthens various parts of his body with repetitive in-place exercises!

5. VISUALIZATION. Use the illustrations to visualize the skills and practice them with a sense of this "perfect" image. Your body can "memorize" the images to gain a better feel for the skills.

SLIDING

Skiers slide on skis in what I call the "All-Purpose Sports Stance." The upper body is upright, the legs are flexed (bent) at the ankles and knees, the feet are side by side, the hands are low. Stand flat-footed on the skis with your weight distributed evenly between the heels and toes and between both skis. Above all, the body is relaxed! This "ready for anything" stance allows you to move easily in any direction.

Telemark wizard Dick Hall of the North American Telemark Organization describes this position as the "slump-o-matic." He asks people to stand tall at rigid attention, then relax their muscles and "slump" into the comfortable position that their bones naturally wish to adopt. The pelvis tilts forward as the navel presses toward the backbone.

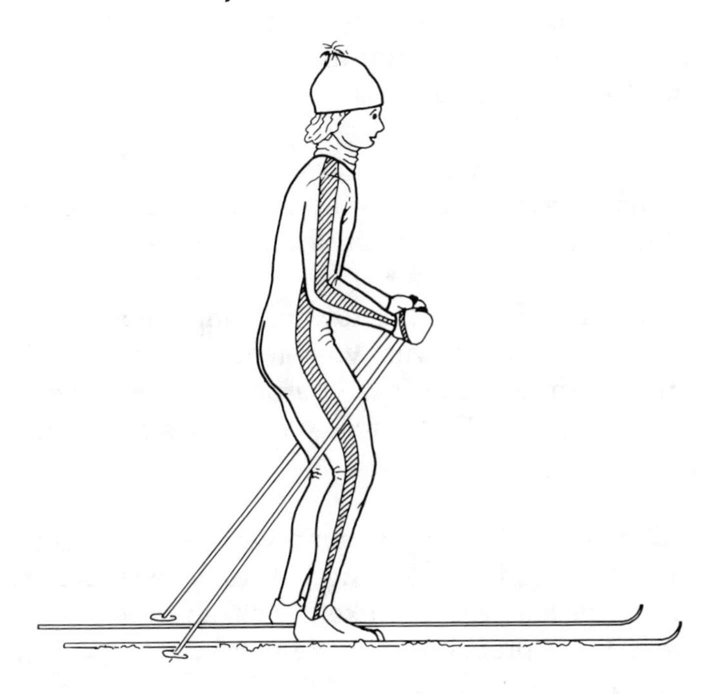

Sliding on skis requires a relaxed, balanced stance—bent legs, an upright, quiet torso, and hands in front of the body.

Practice

Terrain: Flat.

FLAT FEET. Stand flat-footed on your skis. Test the position by gently rocking from your heels to your toes and settling your weight between them. Put your skis together in a narrow parallel stance and rock from side to side; the skis offer little support. Now use a wider parallel stance with the skis as far apart as your shoulders and rock from side to side. This position offers better balance.

LEG FLEXES. Bend your legs so the knees are bent and the ankles press against the tongues of the boots. The knees almost cover the toes. Let the legs "slump" into position several times in a loose, springy fashion. Now close your eyes and drop into position. Check to see if your knees are almost covering your toes.

POPS. Jump into the air and land on your skis without wobbling. Let your legs and ankles bend to absorb the impact. Jump higher and higher and increase the bending to maintain a balanced landing.

GLIDING LEG FLEXES. Take a few running steps and slide on the skis in the all-purpose stance with your feet side by side. Settle into a slumped position with flexed legs as you ride out the glide. Repeat until you can glide comfortably. Then test your balance by sliding down a gentle incline.

STICKS AND SPRINGS. Experiment with a straight-legged stance (sticks) and a bent-legged one (springs). Which feels better? The bent stance where the flexed legs act like shock absorbers should. Feeling wobbly? Your legs are probably stiff. Remember to "go low" with the bent-legged stance!

BALANCE TEST. Try this test with an understanding friend. Stand side by side and try to push each other off balance. Aggressive pushing cannot unbalance a skier who has a flexed, relaxed body stance and skis in a wider stance. But stiffen the legs for an instant and your partner wins.

Problem	Solution
Poor balance (stiff legs)	Bend the knees *and the ankles* to absorb the bumps.
Poor balance (waving hands)	Quiet the hands by placing them on your thighs *and* flex your legs.
Falling forward (bent at the waist)	Keep the torso upright with your buttocks tucked under your shoulders.
Falling sideways (skis too close together)	Widen the basic stance until your feet are under your shoulders.
Falling backward (body too high and weight on heels)	Again, bend the knees and the ankles to lower your center of gravity and move your weight toward your toes. Stand flat-footed. If your back is arched, tilt your pelvis to relax your stance.

GLIDING ON ONE SKI

The key to dynamic skiing is gliding on one ski. The farther a skier can glide on one ski, the more powerful and graceful the skiing style. It takes commitment to balance completely over one ski and "ride" it, but mastering the skill moves a skier beyond the initial shuffling stage to more advanced skiing.

Keeping the leg flexed at the knee and ankle improves balance. Also helpful is the "toe-knee-nose" rule! Aligning each of those body parts above the ski helps to center the entire body and prevent it from falling sideways.

Many skiers have one leg that is dominant, and a good goal is to develop each leg equally. I believe this skill is the single most important ingredient that is missing from the skiing of people who are having difficulties.

Repeat each of these exercises with the weaker leg.

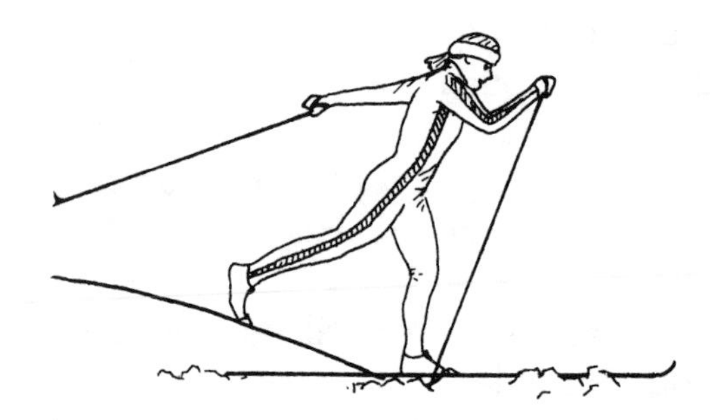

Gliding on one ski is the most difficult skill in cross country skiing.

Practice

Terrain: Flat.

TOE-KNEE-NOSE. Stand on one ski with a flexed leg. Line up your toes, knees, and nose over the ski. You may need to extend your arms to maintain good balance, but keep them low. One side may feel better than the other! (Your dominant leg is often the same leg you use to kick a ball.)

FLEXION-EXTENSION. Straighten the leg and sink into a relaxed position on one ski. The knee almost covers the toes. Develop rhythmic up-and-down movement with each leg.

HOPS. Hop from ski to ski and try to hold each position until you are completely centered over the ski.

ONE-LEGGED LEAPS. Hop on one ski and bend the knee and ankle to keep your balance. When you leap higher, bend the leg more to land smoothly.

BLIND BALANCE. Balance on one leg with closed eyes and focus on your foot. Stay flat-footed by bending the ankle and knee.

ONE-LEGGED BALLET. Stand on one ski with a flexed leg and slide the other ski backward, to the side, and forward. Extend the leg higher in each position and watch how your upper body compensates. For instance, as you slide the leg backward, your body begins to lean forward.

ONE-SKI SCOOTERS. Take off one ski. Push off as if you were on a scooter and ride the ski as far as possible. "Scooter" down a track or use an obstacle course to turn corners.

GLIDING SCOOTERS. Vary the tempo of the "scooters." Gradually slow the tempo so you are gliding longer on the ski.

Terrain: Gentle hill.

RUDDERS. Wearing both skis, descend a gentle incline and balance on one ski. Let the other ski touch the snow briefly, if necessary, to improve balance. But strive to eliminate this "rudder." Repeat with the other leg.

Problem	**Solution**
Falling forward or backward (stiff leg)	Flex the leg at the ankle and knee to let the leg act as a shock absorber. The lower stance drops the center of gravity and increases stability.
Falling sideways	Keep the toes, knee, and nose aligned over the ski. Shift your weight completely to one ski. Full commitment centers your body. A partial weight shift makes you fall to the inside.

Dominant leg	Keep developing strength in the weaker leg by repeating the one-ski exercises.

MOVING FROM SKI TO SKI

Transferring weight from ski to ski is a subtle, more difficult skill, and it is the essence of moving forward. Skiers need a crisp, complete weight transfer to move beyond walking (where both skis shuffle on the snow)

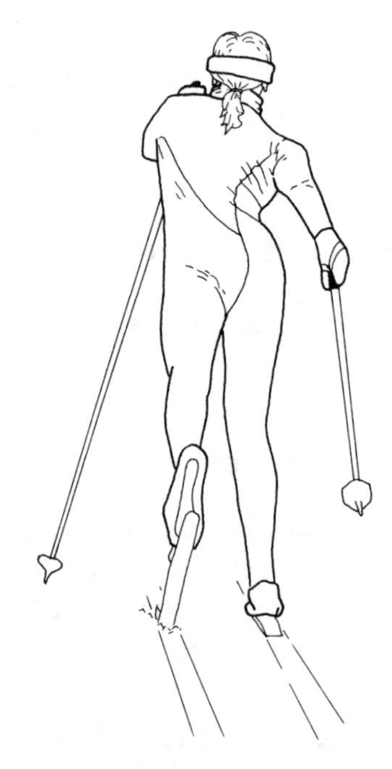

The skier moves her body completely over each ski when she *transfers weight* from ski to ski.

to striding (where one ski at a time glides smoothly along the snow).

Solid weight transfer depends upon good one-ski glide, and you'll benefit from practicing those exercises first. A person with poor balance often straddles the skis and keeps both skis firmly on the snow. An intermediate skier may transfer weight prematurely in the diagonal stride with a telltale slap of the ski as it hits the track early.

That slapping sound is often why new skiers are motivated to seek help. They tell me that they know something is wrong because they're working too hard to keep moving. Weight transfer occurs when the feet are side by side; observing this transition zone keeps you centered over one ski and able to move completely onto the new ski and stay centered over it. It's a rewarding challenge to commit the weight fully to each ski and *at the right time* when moving forward.

Practice

Terrain: Flat.

SNOW TOUCHES. Stand on one ski, then lift it as soon as the other touches the snow. Practice quick transfers from ski to ski. Only one ski on the snow at a time!

SLOW-MOTION TABLEAUX. Slow the tempo. Shift your body completely over each ski (the "toe-knee-nose" rule) and hold each position.

RUNNING IN PLACE. Vary the tempo from a quick jog to a slow-motion pace. Keep the legs flexed and springy for good balance.

GENTLE RUNNING. Run in place "quietly" to dampen up-and-down bobbing. Angle your head and the rest of your body down the track as if you are sending all your energy in that direction rather than in staying upright (with your energy bobbing up toward the sky).

STARTING LINE. Project your body forward like a runner leaving the starting line and jog gently down the track. Let your arms swing naturally.

STEP-OVERS. Stride along a series of obstacles in a line, such as bamboo poles, a rope, or a groomed track. Step over the line and keep striding. Step over the obstacle again. Start on the other side of the line (so the other foot leads the stepping over) and repeat. This exercises forces a skier to stand on each foot while moving.

Terrain: Gentle hill.

RACE WALKING. "Walk" down the hill with short, quick steps while gliding.

STEP-OVERS. Repeat the "Step-Over" exercise on a very gentle hill. The hill increases your speed and affects your balance, so choose a small one. Be ready to ski off the course away from the line if you get unbalanced.

Problem	**Solution**
Shuffling	Remove a ski to eliminate the temptation to use both! Repeat one-ski exercises for improved balance.
Falling forward	Check your upper-body position and eliminate "hinging," or bending over at the waist. Raise the shoulders and move the buttocks forward.

Falling backward	Flex the legs to lower your center of gravity. A "too-tall" stance often topples a skier backward. Project your entire body forward slightly.

PUSHING OFF

Pushing off (or gripping the snow) is also necessary to move forward. Each time a skier steps forward onto one ski, he pushes off the other ski and presses it against the snow. The wax or patterned base on the ski bites into the snow and good traction is the result.

Pushing off is what some skiers call the "kick" in cross-country skiing. Contrary to the image of kicking a ball, the "kicking" leg is the one gripping the snow, providing a firm platform from which to transmit the

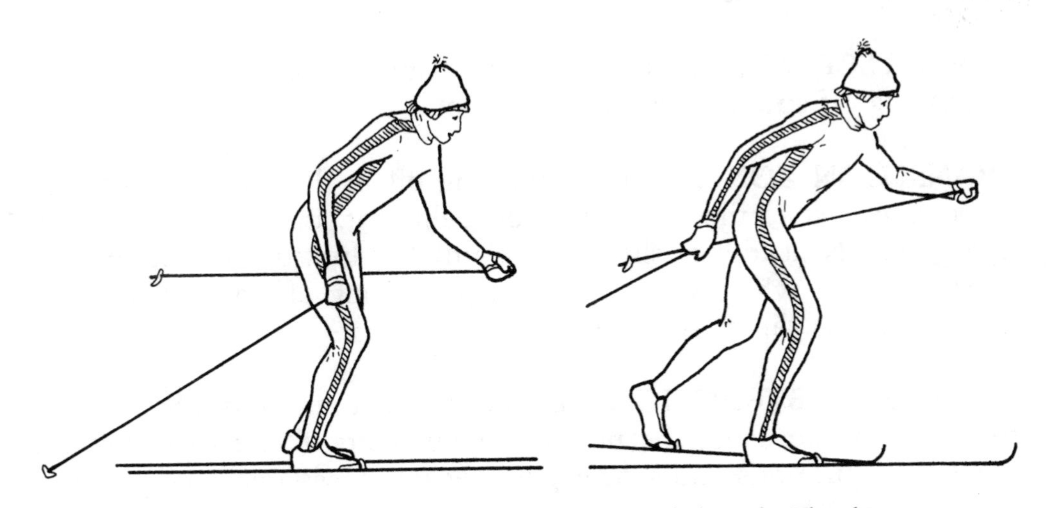

Effective *push-off* occurs when the feet are side by side. The skier can push down with one foot to obtain good traction which allows him to move forward onto the other ski.

power forward. The kicking leg bends a bit (like loading a spring), then extends forward to propel skiers onto their gliding ski. Effective kick is a natural action—like stepping forward—without straining, slipping, or kicking backward.

Pushing off can also be performed on an edged ski. In this case, the sharp corner of the ski provides the firm platform from which to push off. The skier then moves forward in a diagonal direction away from the ski. This kind of push-off can give you more explosive power because the ski edge provides a very stable base. Get ready for the burst of speed!

Practice

Terrain: Flat.

SKI JUMPER. Stand with your feet side by side and lean forward from the ankles (like a ski jumper). Your natural response is stepping forward by pushing off the other foot.

ONE-SKI SCOOTERS. Take off one ski and "scooter" down the track by pushing off strongly with the free foot.

TRANSITION ZONE. Practice pushing off in different places when scootering: next to the "gliding" foot, behind it, in front of it. Which feels better? Next to it or slightly forward! The best traction occurs in a transition zone where your feet overlap. Pushing off too far back can make your skis slip or slap the track.

PUSH-OFF SUBTRACTION. Establish a start and finish. Scooter between them and count the number of push-offs. Strive to reduce the number of push-offs and longer glide results. Does one foot give you better push-off?

FLAT-FOOTED SKIING. Ski down the track with a flat-footed stance when gliding on each ski. As you push off, feel the heel rise over the toes until the toes are pointed. This encourages more powerful pushing off by using the entire foot, from heel to toe.

Problem	**Solution**
Slipping	Make sure the skis are waxed properly for the conditions. Bending from the waist also causes slipping. Stand more upright so the entire body is projected forward in a straight diagonal line.
Slapping	Poor one-legged balance forces you to step back onto the trailing ski too early, and the ski slaps in the track. Standing up too straight also can make the ski slap the track. Repeat one-legged gliding exercises with attention to the basic stance: legs flexed, body projected forward. Also repeat the pushing-off exercises with attention to good push-off in the transition zone.

POLING

Poling is most commonly used to generate speed, and it functions as a rhythmic timing device that helps to coordinate and balance skiers' actions. The arms often push in a pendulum arc: From an initial pole-plant with hands forward of the body, the poling extends downward past the legs and behind the body. The long poles facilitate a lengthy, powerful push across the snow.

Two types of poling are common. *Double poling* occurs when both arms are synchronized and the poles are planted simultaneously. *Alternate poling,* where one pole is planted a time, is just like the arm

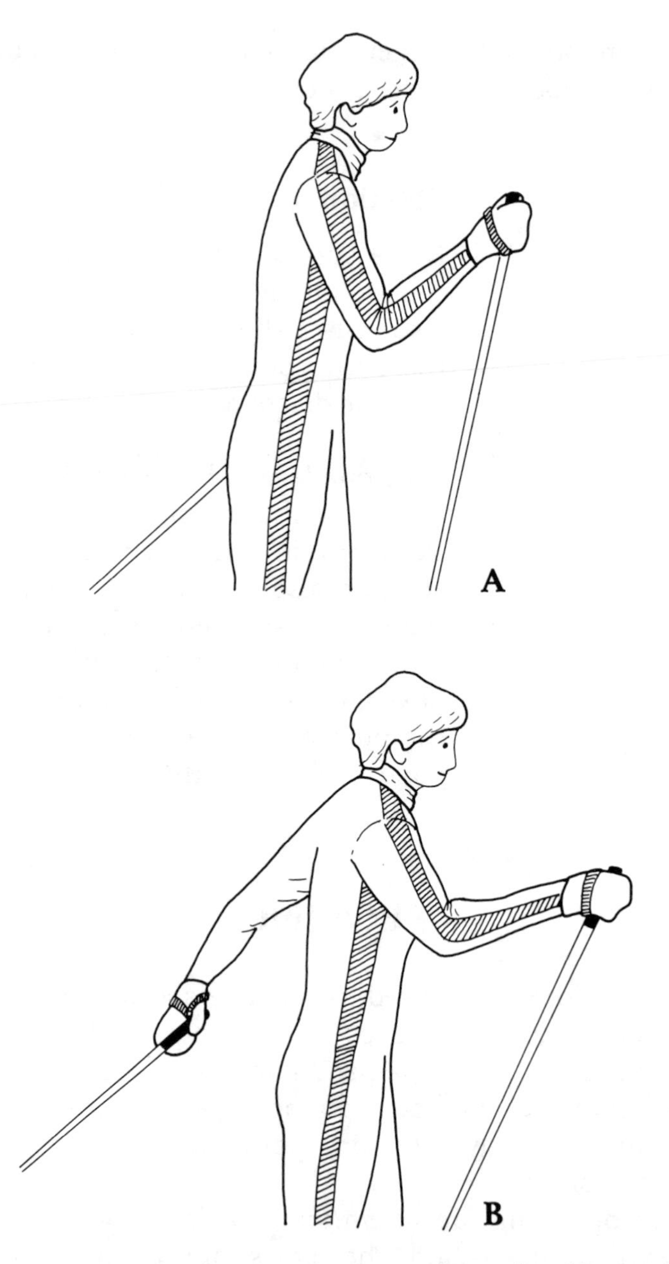

A skier *poles* with a bent arm for more power when beginning to move and an extended arm when gliding smoothly.

swing that occurs in walking or running.

Poling is the least of a new skier's worries, and I favor the elimination of poles if your skiing becomes too mechanical or if you use the poles like crutches. Throwing away the crutches makes you use your legs more effectively and improves your balance. Then you're ready to re-introduce the poles and use them in a more relaxed fashion.

In both types of poling, the arms are bent for more power when beginning the poling, and they tend to straighten with increasing speed. A completely straight arm, however, puts the arm in a mechanically weak position; the contracted muscles of a bent arm are more powerful.

Now skiers use longer poles for greater power, and the length affects the position of the pole-plants and the nature of the pendulum swing. These changes are discussed in the sections on specific techniques.

A relaxed grip on the pole helps to develop tension-free skiing; a tight grip tenses the entire arm and sometimes the body. On the follow-through, the hand can almost but not quite release the pole. Let the thumb and forefinger grip the shaft gently through this phase. Adjust the pole strap so the top of the pole nestles in the V of the thumb and forefinger; this position helps to keep the pole controlled near the hand without being too tight or too loose.

Poles can also be dragged against the snow to slow a skier on hills. Both poles are held together at their grips and braced against the front of the body while the baskets drag behind in the snow.

Double Poling Practice

Terrain: Flat; gentle hill if the snow is slow.

ARM WHIPS. Without using poles, extend the arms forward at shoulder level, swing them downward, brush past the knees, and extend them backward. To move the hands past the knees, you must bend over from the waist, as if bowing. Touch the hands together behind your back to make sure you have extended far enough. Now whip your arms past your body. This crisp whipping will create snappy poling. Now try it when planting the poles.

ANGLED POLE-PLANTS. The baskets are positioned at the feet or behind them, depending upon the length of your poles. (The longer the poles, the farther the baskets land behind your feet.) Push down on the poles to propel you forward. Swing the arms forward, letting the baskets drag along the snow, and plant the poles when your hands reach shoulder level again.

BOWING. Repeat the Angled Pole-Plant exercise. Push on the poles and bend forward from the waist. Let your heavy upper body add extra power to the poling. This addition prevents your arms from tiring too quickly. Contract the stomach muscles as you bow (as in a sit-up), and the poling becomes crisp and powerful.

SUPER BOWS. Concentrate on bowing deeply while double poling. The deeper the bow and the stronger the push against the poles, the longer the glide. Be sure to look down the track when bowing.

Alternate Poling Practice

Terrain: Flat.

ARM PUMPS. Without using poles, swing both arms alternately. "Pump" hard with the arms and increase the tempo. Then slow down the rhythm. Keep varying the tempo. Pumping usually bends the arms more, while a slower tempo extends them in a more flowing fashion.

ALTERNATE POLE-PUSHES. Keep both feet side by side and propel yourself down the track by alternate poling. This is a good workout! (Don't try it in new, slow snow.) Extending each arm behind the body increases your power and glide.

MID-POLE SWINGS. Ski down the track, and hold your poles at midlength in the air. Swing your arms and keep the poles in alignment with your skis. Don't let the poles cross over the skis. (Pole swings should be parallel to the gliding skis.)

POLE DRAGS. Ski down the track as if you are jogging, and use alternate poling to propel you forward. Swing the arms naturally and let the poles drag on the snow without pushing against them. Gradually increase the pressure against the pole when each arm reaches the forward position—gently at first, then a little harder. This exercise stresses relaxed, rhythmic arm motion rather than hard pushing against the poles. Make sure the arms swing behind your body for a good follow-through.

Problem	Solution
Poor timing	Timing is more often a problem with alternate poling. A stiffened stance is apparent, and the poles appear to be used as crutches. Loosen up the legs with a springy, exaggerated stride down the track to develop a noticeable rhythm. Loosen your grip; use the Pole Drag drill. Try poling up a hill.
Lack of extension	Extend the poling behind the body. With double poling, touch the hands together behind your back to exaggerate the extension. With alternate poling, extend each arm backward, let go of the pole, open the hand fully, and point the forefinger backward (rather than down at the ground).

EDGING

Edging is the way the bottom corner of the ski digs or bites into the snow. Skiers use edging primarily to control their skis when turning, slowing down, or stopping. The greater the tilt of the ski, the deeper it digs into the snow and the greater the edging. This increased resistance against the snow creates drag that slows the skier.

This skill is important to people who have problems with speed control. It's the most common request from students in ski lessons, and they ask for advice about how to slow down! We practice the basics of edging on flat terrain first and take the mystery out of this simple skill. Don't expect to learn this skill on a hill.

The more skiers use their upper and lower bodies independently, the more proficient their edging becomes. If the legs swing to one side to edge the skis, then the torso should counterbalance by leaning the other way. (The upper body still appears relatively erect; it shouldn't lean over from the waist.) The body is now angulated along its length, but the skier's weight remains over the feet to apply pressure to the skis.

Edging is also a part of skating, but skiers use their bodies differently. The leg and torso remain relatively straight and aligned, and skiers use the edge of the ski to project themselves forward. The leg might coil a little at the outset, like a spring, but then it straightens to provide the push.

Practice

Terrain: Flat.

FOOT ROLLS. Keep the skis parallel in a wide, secure stance, the feet in line with the shoulders. Roll the feet and knees in the same direction (to the left or right) to edge the skis. Then roll the feet the other way. A smooth, rhythmic swinging of the knees below the upper body develops good edging.

A skier *edges* the ski with a straight leg when skating.

BIG AND LITTLE BITES. Vary the degree of edging. Edge gently, then deeply. Watch how softly and strongly the skis bite into the snow. Watch the difference in how far your knees swing.

GIANT STEPS. Take a giant step sideways and move your body over the ski. Then shift it over the other ski. Roll from edge to edge and feel the stretch along the inside of your legs.

A skier uses bent and angulated legs when controlling turns with edging.

ROCKING Vs. Stand with the skis in a V-shape, the tails slanted together. Rock from ski to ski and watch the edges dig into the snow.

Terrain: Moderate hill.

SIDESLIPPING. Stand sideways across the hill. Roll your feet down the hill to release the edges, and skid downhill. Stop the ski by edging again. Your knees should also move away from the hill (to skid) and into it (to edge). Repeat from the top, but face in the other direction. You may find that one leg feels more secure in "leading" the skid.

TRAVERSES. Ski on a diagonal line across a hill and edge the skis (knees into the hill) to prevent slideslipping. Try a steeper hill that requires greater edging.

SIDESLIP TRAVERSES. Repeat the traverse, releasing the edges (knees away from the hill) to slideslip slightly. Stop the slideslip by edging. Then traverse the hillside with intermittent sideslipping. A steeper hill tests your newfound control.

ONE-SKI TRAVERSES. Glide across the hill on the downhill ski, using the uphill ski when necessary to regain balance. Then glide on the uphill ski. Keep the legs flexed, the foot flat on the ski.

Problem	Solution
Extreme edging	Old boots or weak ankles let the feet roll off the ski and drag on the snow. Keep the feet as flat as possible on the ski and roll them gently to hold a moderate edge.
Banking	Skiers lean their entire bodies to edge the skis (and often fall). Use the upper and lower body independently. Let the legs bend and swing beneath the torso to edge the skis.

SKIDDING

A skidded ski moves sideways or around against the snow. Skiers brush the skis across the snow by pushing with their legs. Relaxed,

Skidding the skis is aided by raising the body to release ski pressure against the snow and lowering the body to increase pressure.

flexed legs exert pressure against the ski; it's difficult to begin or control skidding with stiff legs.

Skidding is the first skill that moves a skier away from a forward direction. As a result, the sideways movement can be disconcerting at the beginning. Practice develops smooth and satisfying skidding—especially for those who like to "swoosh" their skis to a stop.

Exercise both legs equally to develop consistent skidding. A dominant leg can inhibit a skier's ability to turn easily in both directions.

Practice

Terrain: Flat.

RIDGES. Push one ski sideways several times. Push with the entire foot. Watch the ridge of snow that forms and try to keep the ridge parallel to your other ski. Using the entire foot helps to do this. Pushing with just the toes creates uneven ridges.

PRESSURE RIDGES. Vary the pressure against the ski. Light pressure creates a small ridge, heavy pressure builds a big one. What happens to your leg? It bends more when you push harder.

ANGLED RIDGES. Skid one ski at an angle to the other one; point the tip of the skidded ski toward the other ski. Push the skidded ski sideways as well as around by rotating the foot and leg.

HOPS. Keep the skis parallel, and hop from side to side. Let the skis float across the snow at first, then gradually increase the pressure against the snow at the end of each hop to skid the ski the last few inches.

Terrain: Gentle hill.

STEP DOWNS. Stand sideways across a gentle incline. Keep the uphill ski stationary and skid the downhill ski farther down the hill. Bring the other ski next to it. Continue to take small skidding steps sideways. Repeat the exercise with larger skidding steps down the hill.

SIDESLIP TRAVERSES. Ski across the hill, release the edges of the skis, and slip sideways. Concentrate on more skidding and less edging.

Problem	**Solution**
Edging	The ski digs excessively into the snow as if it were on a train rail, or intermittently to unbalance the skier. Roll the ankles and knees under the body more to flatten the ski to eliminate the extreme edge. Keep the legs and ankles flexed to press gently

against the ski with the entire foot and skid it more easily across the snow.

Limited power	Stiff legs have little power to push the ski across the snow. Bend the legs at the ankle and knee so that you create power when extending the leg.

STEERING

Steering is the rotary action of the leg and foot that turns a ski. Pivoting the legs will turn the feet that are attached to the skis! Because steering begins with the toes and finishes with the force of the entire leg, skiers who steer only with their knees may encounter difficulty with steering.

Steering is the most subtle of the basic skills, and it is usually used in conjunction with other skills, like skidding and edging, to turn a ski. However, the absence of steering is usually what causes a turn to fail, and skiers who finally feel the effects of strong steering understand what a good turn can be like. When skiers *skid* their skis less and *steer* their skis more, they move from the realm of intermediate to more advanced skiing.

This skill is crucial for skiers with inconsistent turns. It helped me to clearly understand the dynamics of turning, and since I've focused on it in instruction, the success rate among my students has skyrocketed.

Practice

Terrain: Flat.

BIG-TOE PRESSES. Stand in place and plant a ski pole between the tips of the skis. Lift one ski and rotate it like a blade on a helicopter until it presses against the pole. Feel how the big toe presses against the boot.

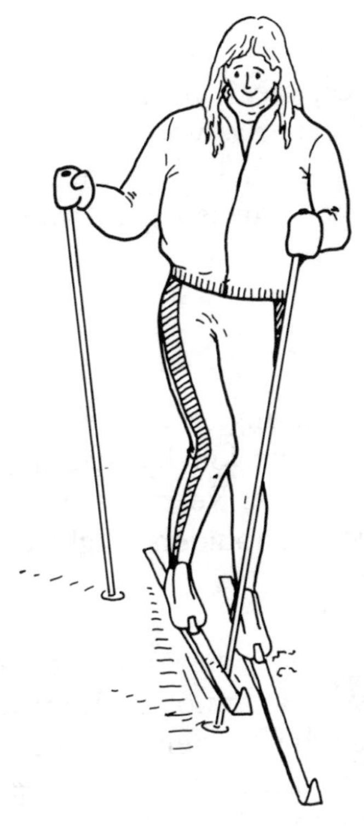

Steering is a subtle skill where the skier rotates the foot, knee and hip to turn the ski. Pressing the ski against the pole lets you feel how the leg steers the ski.

BIG-TOE TURNS. Repeat the exercise, but keep the ski on the ground. Rotate it across the snow and press the tip against the pole.

KNEES PLEASE. Repeat the Big-Toe Turn exercise, but let the knee press toward the pole. This action adds extra strength to the steering.

PIGEON TOES. From a crouched parallel stance, hop upward to lift the skis slightly off the snow and steer both skis into an A shape (like a snowplow). You'll feel pigeon-toed with the tips together and the tails apart. Next time, lift your weight just enough to slide the skis into position without lifting them off the snow.

TANDEM TOE TURNS. Try this one with a partner. Let your partner (who isn't wearing skis) push you across the snow by pushing against your hips. When you have a steady pace, steer your skis into the A position. Let your partner push faster and faster as you continue to steer your skis. Steer more strongly with one leg, then the other one. Steer your big toe in the direction you wish to go. This is a great way to learn to steer before you reach the hills!

Problem	**Solution**
Upper-body swing	The torso is rotating to force the turn. Make the leg do its job by steering with the big toe and knee. Keep the torso quiet and swivel your shoulders slightly away from the turn.
Extreme edging	The ski is edged so strongly that it digs into the snow and cannot be moved. Roll the ski flat. Use the Tandem Toe Turns and follow a straight course with no edging. Re-experience good sliding across the snow before trying to steer with your big toe.
Little or no steering	You're probably trying to turn with your knee rather than your toes. Point the toe strongly in the direction that you wish to turn. Let the steering develop from the feet first.

Once these skills feel comfortable, the next step is blending them into various maneuvers that enable skiers to handle cross-country terrain. But don't be afraid to return to these exercises at any point. Even racers return to warm-up exercises to maintain their skills and eliminate the "glitches" that sneak into their skiing.

Videotaping is an invaluable aid in improving your skiing. If you feel that your skiing is inefficient, you need to watch yourself and analyze your moves with the help of an experienced skier or instructor. Although I have been teaching skiing for a decade, I make sure that my skiing is videotaped each year. It's amazing what can creep into your style just when you think perfection has been reached!

Classical Cross-Country Skiing

4

The traditional moves in cross-country skiing are the best place for skiers to begin their practice. Simply walking, shuffling, or striding gets you moving quickly and oriented to the balance needed to glide on these skinny skis. Groomed tracks at a cross-country ski area are a good place to begin. The tracks direct the skis in a straight line and let you concentrate on other elements of the moves. Once you develop a basic proficiency with the moves, then untracked snow is a good experience.

Many people tell me in ski lessons that they wished they had begun skiing at a cross-country ski area. Intrigued by the opportunity to simply ski from their back doors, they (or other members of their family) experienced frustration in breaking their own trails. They were amazed at how the groomed tracks made skiing so much easier and improved their styles dramatically. It prepared them for a more enjoyable experience at the local golf course or park.

USING THE ACTIVITIES

These tips can make the exercises enjoyable and rewarding:

1. PROBLEM IDENTIFICATION. Problems with a ski move are caused by poor development of a basic skill. Identify the skill and return to the exercises in the previous chapter that improve the skill. Each move has a "Problem and Solution" section to help improve your skiing.

2. FREE SKIING. Taking a break is often important because it clears the head and relaxes the body. Free skiing or games with friends are excellent diversions and lead to more good practice.

3. FOLLOW THE LEADER. Mimicking a good skier is an effective way to learn for those who need to watch a move to understand it. Skiing behind model skiers is an excellent tool.

4. SYNCHRONIZED SKIING. Matching a skier's pace works well for those who need to perform a move to understand it. Skiing beside better skiers and synchronizing the action helps you to push your limits.

It's common for people who ski together to develop a similar style. I ski like the relative from whom I learned, and I'm glad that person is a superb skier! Several instructors at my ski school resemble me because I originally taught them to ski. It's a very effective way of learning, but be sure to pick a good model!

DIAGONAL STRIDE

The diagonal stride, an action similar to walking or running, is the most common Nordic move and the essence of classical skiing. Gliding smoothly on skis in the diagonal stride is every skier's desire, and the ability to ride the gliding ski separates the beginning skier from the intermediate.

The term "diagonal" refers to the opposing action of arms and legs that occurs naturally when people walk or run. Because analyzing this opposing action tends to tense skiers and destroy their natural rhythms, the practice activities focus initially on elements that encourage coordinated rhythm. Shorter strides with a faster tempo at the outset establish a good rhythm and keep skiers balanced on their skis. Otherwise, beginners tend to wobble down the track, fighting to keep their balance.

Once you develop a sense of rhythm, however, you should focus on the various skills that develop more powerful striding. The most important underlying skill is the ability to glide on one ski without losing one's balance. The longer the glide, the more flowing the diagonal stride. Another important element is pushing off at the right moment when the feet are side by side. Otherwise, the skis exhibit an annoying tendency to slip and slap.

You can become a victim of mechanical practice with the diagonal stride. In striving to lengthen glide, avoid a focus on an extension of the rear leg. Forcefully lifting or extending the leg is a strain that can actually undermine the desire to balance longer on the gliding ski. The leg rises naturally as a result of the skier pushing off and moving forward. Too many people strive for the posed magazine image at the expense of efficient skiing. Let it happen naturally.

Practice

Skills: Gliding on one ski, moving from ski to ski, pushing off, poling.

Terrain: Flat, tracked.

BASIC STANCE. Practicing the basic stance in a stationary position can be a valuable balance exercise. The body is centered over the skis, not behind them. Stand on one leg with the foot directly beneath or slightly behind the knee; flex the knee and ankle to balance solidly. The foot and knee are just beneath the chest area. The back leg is extended comfortably off the ground and is counterbalanced by the head and arm out front. Use your poles to maintain balance when you lean the body forward slightly. Don't bend at the waist.

Return to a neutral position, close your eyes, settle into the basic stance, then check the position. Recreational skiers use a more upright stance, while racers project their bodies farther forward. Experiment with moving the hips and chest farther forward until you start to fall forward. This gives you a sense of how racing skiers hurtle their bodies down the tracks.

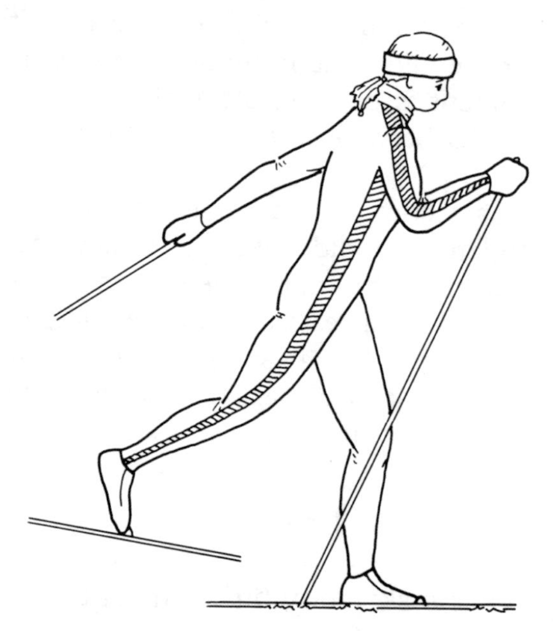

The skier varies her posture in the *diagonal stride* for touring, recreational skiing and racing. A touring skier uses a more upright stance.

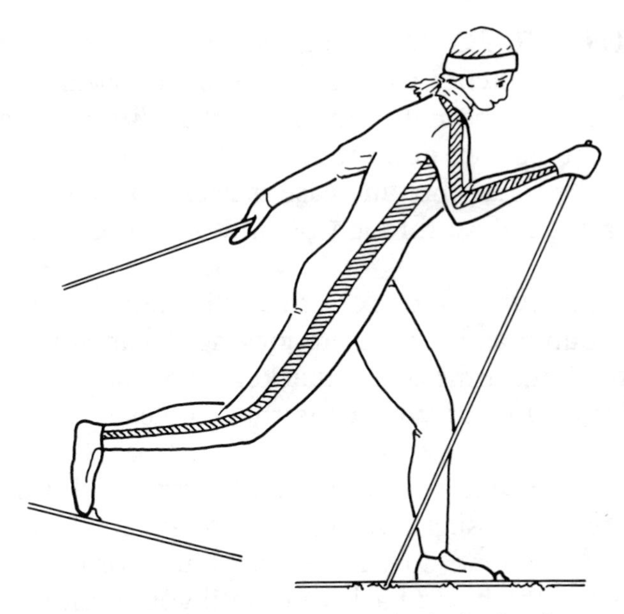

A recreational skier projects her body farther forward to glide better.

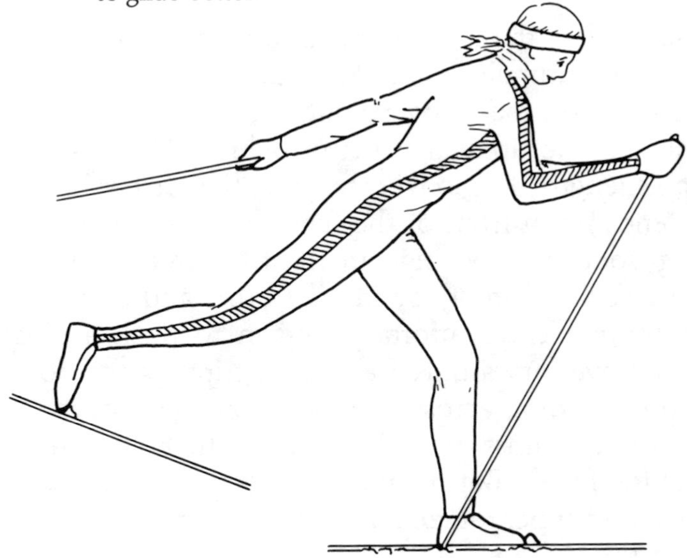

A racer leans diagonally forward to propel herself aggressively down the track.

SKIING WITHOUT POLES. This useful exercise prevents you from using the poles as crutches to improve balance. Swing your arms naturally when striding. (The right arm and left leg work together, then the left arm and right leg. But don't think about this coordination.) Begin by walking down the track, then increase the tempo to glide briefly on each ski. Let your arms follow through behind your body naturally.

JOGGING. Ski down the track with a quick tempo, using short strides. Let your arms pump as if you were jogging. Change to a running pace, and watch how your arms pump quicker. Vary the tempo between running and jogging. Do this with or without poles.

ARM SWINGS. Swing your arm parallel with each ski without crossing over the ski. (Crossing over can rotate your torso and undermine balance.) Point your hand down the track ahead of the ski tips, swing it down past the midthigh and backward until you point your fingers at the track behind your skis.

POLE DRAGS. Wear the pole straps around the wrists like a bracelet, and swing the arms naturally while skiing down the track. The poles can drag along the snow on the recovery until the arm is raised high enough to gently plant the pole tip at the feet or behind. (The exact spot varies according to pole length. The longer the pole, the farther behind the foot. If the pole tip ends up in front of the feet, the pole may be too short or you are raising your arm too high in front.) Don't apply any pressure against the pole at first; simply swing the arms and stride forward.

After the rhythm feels comfortable, begin to push against the pole straps gently to move forward. Refrain from gripping the pole. Continue to allow the pole to drag across the snow on the recovery. Gradually increase the pushing against the poles and eventually grip the poles with the thumb and forefinger. But maintain gentle pressure. The emphasis is a relaxed arm swing synchronized with the striding rather than a strong pushing against the poles.

ANKLE POPS. In a stationary position, bend your ankles as you step from ski to ski. A bouncy, exaggerated motion results. Stride down the track with increased bend in the ankles when pushing off the ski. This spring from the ankles puts more power forward onto the gliding ski. Then pop more subtly from ski to ski to remove excessive bobbing—a little is fine as long as your entire body heads forward down the track. An upright, bobbing stance sends the power into sky and should be avoided.

As you balance on the forward gliding ski, your ankle straightens. However, the supporting leg remains flexed at the knee.

DIAGONAL STRIDE SUBTRACTION. Ski in an easy fashion along a track between two points and count the number of strides. Try to reduce the number of strides in subsequent passes. At first it's easy to subtract many strides off the original total, but it becomes more difficult as you continue. Experiment with pushing off harder and using stronger arm swings to develop longer gliding.

TANDEM DRIBBLING. Ski across groomed snow with a friend and pass a ball back and forth. This activity develops good one-ski balance when you pass the ball. Be ready for much falling and laughing.

HIP SWIVELS. Loosen the pelvic area and rotate the pelvis when moving from ski to ski. This rotation of the hips around the spine helps skiers shift their weight completely over the gliding ski. It also provides a greater forward thrust onto the gliding ski and lengthens the glide.

HEEL GLIDE. Experiment with keeping your weight nearer your heels when riding the glide ski. (Some weight remains on the ball of the foot or you will fall backward.) The ski tip lightens, rides up over snow more easily, and helps to maintain good speed. Guard against shifting your body backward; keep it centered over the ski, knee under the chest, and the lower leg almost perpendicular to the ground.

Problem	Solution
Shuffling	Shuffling is often necessary at the beginner level to get skiers moving. But beyond the introductory level it interferes with good skiing. Skiers who shuffle need the security of both feet on the ground. Practice one-ski exercises to improve the ability to glide on one foot. Use a jogging tempo with its shorter strides to enhance balance. Also refer to the exercises for moving from ski to ski.
Inefficient stance	The torso can be either too upright or too bent over; as a result, body weight remains behind the forward foot when you attempt to glide. The key factor is getting the hips farther forward so you can ride the gliding ski comfortably. Also beware of straightening the gliding leg, which forces you to push off sooner and shortens glide; keep the leg flexed at the knee.
Slapping	The ski hits the track too soon in the back when skiers transfer their weight prematurely. An upright stance here contributes to poor balance on the gliding ski. Move the hips forward and the chest over the knee. Use the practice exercises to improve these two skills: moving from ski to ski and pushing off.
Slipping	When you wait too long to push off, the feet move too far apart and you can't set the wax to get good traction. Pushing off

	should occur when the feet are side by side or nearly so—at midpoint in the stride. Use the pushing-off practice exercises to rediscover the transition zone. Improper waxing may also be affecting traction.
Poor timing	The striding and poling is uncoordinated. Removing the poles as well as developing a faster tempo may initially help to correct the timing. Use the Pole Drag drill to encourage relaxed poling. Striding uphill also helps correct poor timing.
Blocked hips	A lack of hip rotation interferes with good glide. The leg and foot glide forward, but the hips hang back and stop the momentum. If the upper body comes forward, slipping may result. Use the Hip Swivel exercise to loosen the pelvis.

UPHILL DIAGONAL STRIDE

The uphill diagonal stride is the most powerful way to ascend a hill, but it requires more commitment than do other uphill techniques. It is an intermediate maneuver that skiers may want to try after they have practiced other ski moves, such as the herringbone.

One benefit to the uphill diagonal is its promotion of good timing between the striding and poling. Because the stride is shorter, skiers use a natural running stride and balance is enhanced. If timing is a problem, then skiers should use a steeper hill. However, a hill that forces a skier to use a herringbone is too steep.

The basic stance in the diagonal stride changes subtly to climb hills. As the strides shorten, the poling follow-through also shortens, but the

hands should still pass behind the body for a good thrust.

Stepping up the hill with the entire body is an important concept in the uphill diagonal. As the skier steps forward, the hips must also come forward to keep weight centered over the wax pocket of the ski. Otherwise, skiers feel as if they have to climb up and over the ski to ride it again. Hip rotation helps greatly to prevent slipping.

Successful skiers are aggressive with their bodies on the hills, and once they begin to climb, they keep going with the momentum. Hesitating often causes skiers to stall, and their weight starts to slide behind their feet. Children attack the hill with gusto, and when it gets steeper they shift into overdrive, take shorter steps, and run up the hill.

A good practice area allows a skier to move between flat terrain and a gradual uphill. Being able to crest the hill and continue skiing on flat

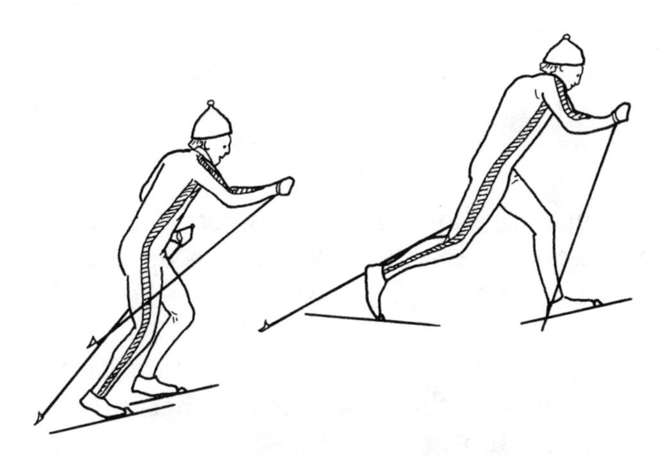

The skier must propel the entire body forward in the *uphill diagonal stride.* Step forward onto a flat foot with good hip rotation, and the rest of the body will follow.

terrain is also valuable. The transitions offer skiers an excellent opportunity to change their tempo from longer strides on the flats to shorter strides on the hills.

Practice

Skills: Gliding on one ski, moving from ski to ski, pushing off, poling.

Terrain: Gradual uphill, tracked or untracked.

CHARGING THE HILL. Run up the hill with short strides while watching the top of the hill. This prevents hunching over and keeps the hips centered over the skis.

TOE GRABS. Climb the hill and slide your foot forward with the toes "grabbing" the snow to gain traction. This technique tends to keep the feet moving up the hill under the body instead of falling behind.

HIP SWIVELS. Loosen the hips to allow the hip to rotate forward with each uphill stride. The rotation keeps the hips moving up the hill and gives more power to the stride. Better glide also occurs.

TIP-HIP PUSHES. Slide your ski uphill and push the ski a little farther by rotating your hip. Keep trying to push the tip an inch farther forward with each step by pushing from the hips.

POWER POLING. As soon as the arm swings forward, plant the pole and push downward against it without hesitating. Use a very bent arm (the forearm is aligned very near the pole) to get started; this "first gear" position provides good power to move. Once you are moving up the hill, the arm position can be modified and extended slightly in "second gear." When you crest the hill and speed builds on the flat terrain, a more extended "third gear" position can be used.

SPINE ON A LINE. Move your body firmly over each ski as you ski uphill. Think of your spine shifting slightly from side to side as you move from ski to ski. Check your head's alignment over the ski; you should be able to look straight down and see the ski directly beneath your body.

Problem	Solution
Straddling	Straddling the skis is a tentative move that prevents solid weight transfer from ski to ski. Step uphill and firmly over each ski to

	center the body. Weight transfer is necessary to help set the wax and to push off effectively. Repeat the Spine on a Line exercise.
Stomping	A running step up the hill is often used on very steep terrain. But stomping uphill sends too much power into the ground on moderate or gradual terrain. Think of sending your power up, up, up the hill by sliding your skis forward. Tip-Hip Pushes can help reduce excessive stomping.
Inefficient striding	See the Diagonal Stride section.

HERRINGBONE

When skiers begin to struggle using the diagonal stride to climb uphill, it's time to shift down into the herringbone. The herringbone is slower, but it gives greater purchase against the snow. Skiers move their skis into a tails-together V and edge their skis to step uphill. They use their poles in an alternating fashion, as in normal uphill walking. I've watched children coach their parents very effectively by saying, "Mom, walk like a duck." The ducklings have the right analogy!

Standing upright keeps the body centered over the skis. Then skis can edge properly to prevent slipping and move up the hill. Watching the top of the hill is helpful. Beginners often step on the tails of their skis because they tend to be timid in stepping far enough up the hill. Step up, up, up the hill.

The basic herringbone has several useful variations. A half herringbone works on easier terrain, where the half-V position lets the skier brake with the angled ski and step uphill more easily with the straight ski. It's

The *herringbone* is a more secure way to climb a steep hill. Notice how the skier steps forward, up the hill, to avoid stepping on the other ski.

also effective when climbing a hill on a diagonal line; use the angled ski on the downhill side and the straight ski steps along the traverse route.

The gliding herringbone is an easier move for skiers who feel comfortable sliding on one ski. As the skiers use the full herringbone to move uphill, they can slide forward onto their skis rather than step. Gliding from ski to ski increases the speed at which skiers climb. Glide is enhanced by moving aggressively from ski to ski and centering the hips over each ski. The hips seem to sashay back and forth.

Practice

Skills: Moving from ski to ski, edging, pushing off, poling, gliding on one ski (gliding herringbone).

Terrain: Gentle to moderate uphill.

BASIC STANCE. Approach a hill by striding, and when the hill steepens, walk the skis into a V shape with the tails together. Then begin stepping up the hill with the skis edged against the snow. Watch the hill's top and step forward to step clear of the other ski.

TRAVERSES. Pick a diagonal route up the hill and use the half herringbone to climb easily.

TACKING. Traverse in zigzag manner uphill, and use a mixture of herringbones and half herringbones to traverse and turn corners.

VARIABLE Vs. Change the V shape from wide to narrow as you climb uphill. Keep your weight centered over your feet as the V gets narrower.

RUN HERRINGBONE. Charge the hill by running in a herringbone. It's a high-energy move, but fast!

GLIDING HERRINGBONE. At the base of a hill, begin to slide the skis into a herringbone and strive to add a few inches to the length of glide of each ski. It's a subtle transition from a herringbone to the gliding version and an easier one if you think of gently sliding from ski to ski. Let your hips sway from side to side as you climb.

Problem	Solution
Slipping	The stance is hunched over and the skier is looking down. Stand upright to keep the weight centered over each foot as you step from ski to ski. Watch the top of the hill.
Clicking tails	The skier is stepping from side to side. Step forward up the hill. Use a wider V for a stronger platform from which to push off and step up.
Stalling (gliding herringbone)	Straddling the skis forces the skier to rock off each ski quickly with limited glide; weight hangs in the middle. Step solidly onto each ski, centering the hips over the ski. The hip movement from ski to ski helps to generate extra glide.

DOUBLE POLE

Although the complexity of the diagonal stride commands much of a skier's attention, double poling is really the move at the heart of cross-country skiing. This versatile maneuver is used in both classical and free-style skiing, and its practice is necessary for skiers who want to learn the newer skating techniques.

Skiers lean forward to move the hips ahead of the feet and push simul-

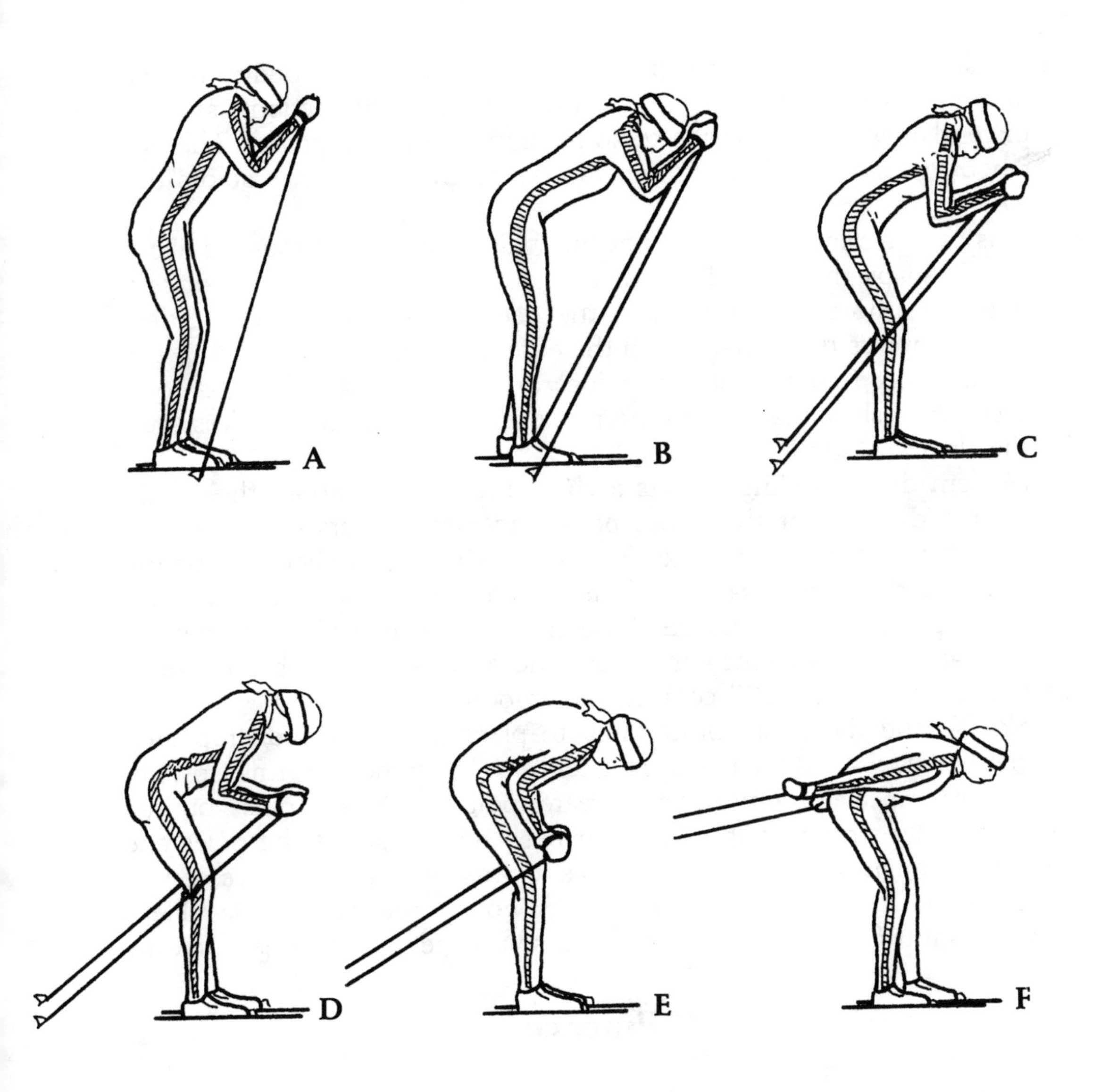

Good power with the *double pole* stems from the skier bending forward (compressing) to lower her weight onto the poles (A–E). The arms extend behind the body for effective poling (F).

taneously against the planted poles. They let their upper bodies follow their arms to give extra power to the pushing. This action uses the stronger, larger muscles of the torso to supplement arm power. The upper body rises and falls in a fluid motion as the skier poles across the snow.

This compression of the torso at the waist tightens the muscles like a sit-up. It snaps the body forward and down to promote crisp double poling. The more power needed, the deeper the compression. Skiers should compress their torsos until they are approximately parallel to the ground. A deep compression provides a longer poling phase for good power. Once skiers have good momentum, they tend to compress their bodies less.

Modern double poling reflects a change in thought about the rigidly coordinated action of the upper body and arms. Skiers once dropped their upper bodies at the same time that their arms pushed against the poles. This rigid coordination of the arms and body provided an initial burst of power that decreased through the glide. Now a more flexible coordination lets different parts move more freely, although the overall arm-body actions are still coordinated smoothly.

Skiers bend the arms comfortably to plant the poles and drop their upper bodies toward the poles. This tends to bring the forearms closer to the poles, especially with today's greater pole length, and puts you in a mechanically strong position to then push down against the poles and follow through behind the body. This approach generates more consistent power throughout the move. As poling progresses, the skier's weight shifts from the toes to the heels so the feet appear to jet forward.

Practice

Skills: Sliding, poling.

Terrain: Flat, gentle downhill if snow conditions are slow.

BASIC STANCE. Begin in an upright position with the hips over the feet, the body relaxed. Swing your hands forward with comfortably bent arms to plant the poles. The longer the poles, the higher your hands (shoulder to head level). Plant the poles at or behind the feet, and push against an angled pole.

The torso drops down toward the poles, and the arms may give slightly to align the forearms near the poles. This bent-arm position lets you push strongly against the poles and follow through with more body compression. The arms extend backward as a natural extension of this compression.

Once the body is parallel to the skis, you ride the sliding skis, straighten the body, and swing the hands back to the plant position. An important benefit here is a relaxation phase that stretches the body and prepares it for the next contraction of muscles. The legs bend a little during double poling to relieve lower back strain, but they are generally straight to provide a stable point from which a skier bends over.

BOWING. Vary the degree of upper-body compression in a series of deep and shallow bows. The deeper the bow, the longer the pole-pushing, the greater the glide.

SIT-UPS. Begin double poling from an upright stance, and contract the stomach muscles sharply to compress the upper body. It's like doing sit-ups in a leaned-over position. Relax the muscles to stand upright again.

THE SKI JUMPER. Raise your arms for the pole plant, and let your hips move forward beyond your feet. You'll feel like a ski jumper when you project your body forward. Moving your body forward helps to build momentum.

ARM POLING. As an experiment, double-pole with just your arms. Then add compression of the torso to feel the added power of these strong muscles. Mark a starting point in a track. Pole with just the arms and mark how far you glided. Then pole with good compression and note the difference in glide.

POWER POLING. Use strongly bent arms (about a ninety-degree angle at the elbow) in "first gear" to get moving, straighten the arms somewhat in "second gear" to maintain momentum, and use slightly bent arms in "third gear" when accelerating down the track.

Find a section of trail with a gentle rise, followed by a slight descent. Double-pole up and over the rise, using the stronger "first gear" position to generate additional power on the uphill. Shift to "third" gear for the descent.

POLE DRAGS. Let the poles drag along the snow while you bring the hands back to the plant position. As soon as the body returns to an upright stance and the hands reach a point between shoulder and head level, push against the poles. The pole tips will land in a location appropriate to their length. The longer the poles, the farther back they land. Pole drags eliminate any excessive lifting of the poles.

SIGHT-SEEING. Double-pole along a track with your eyes on a landmark in the distance. This helps to prevent your head from dropping too much and keeps you anticipating any changes in terrain. When compressing deeply, you probably can't see the landmark, but keep looking past your ski tips.

HEEL GLIDING. Let your weight move closer to your heels after poling to get maximum glide. This action lifts the ski tips slightly to prevent drag against the snow. With crisp compression you may experience the sensation of your heels shooting forward. Again, don't strive for an artificial action; let it happen as a natural reaction to dynamic compression.

DOUBLE-POLE SUBTRACTION. Double-pole in a relaxed manner between two points. Count the number of double-pole actions. In subsequent passes, try to reduce the double poling. Experiment with changes that will produce longer gliding: deeper compressions, bent arms, weight on the heels.

Problem	**Solution**
No compression	Lack of compression stems from poor use of the body; either the skier remains too upright or he is permanently hunched over. This problem often plagues beginner skiers who get fatigued from poling with only the arms. Recapture the rise-and-fall action of the torso with Sit-Ups and Bowing.
Excessive pole lift	Short poles are often a cause. Raising the hands too high lifts the pole tips off the ground before the poles are planted; the skier's power is heading toward the ski rather than down the track. Swing the hands forward and plant the poles immediately when the ski tips are near the feet.
Heel lift	Rising onto the toes occurs when you try to get more leverage by dropping onto the poles. But tippy toes are unstable on sliding skis, and the best power comes from using compressions of the upper body. Stand flat-footed.
Hips too far back	The hips are dragging behind excessively and slowing momentum. (This often accompanies a hunched-over upper body.) Bring the hips forward of the feet in an upright stance when preparing to double-pole. Assume the Ski Jumper position.
Delayed poling	The upper body collapses toward the poles, and the arms fail to begin the poling

until the torso is parallel to the ground. The arms lose the valuable thrust from the compression, and weak poling results. Once compression begins and moves the forearms toward the poles, the arms are in their strongest position to push against the poles. Don't hesitate at this point; use the torso power to help whip the poles behind the legs.

KICK DOUBLE POLE

The kick double pole evolves naturally from the double pole when the skier's momentum begins to slow. It combines double poling with a leg push to thrust the skier forward. The skier uses more energy to get moving, but the move functions like booster rockets to maintain good momentum. The kick double pole and the double pole are often used interchangeably to handle changes in terrain.

The kick occurs when the feet are under the skier's body and the arms are moving forward after poling. As the hands return past the legs, the skier pushes off one foot (ski) and glides onto the forward ski. The supporting leg is flexed.

The pushing-off occurs downward to set the wax and provides a momentary base from which to push the skier forward. As the kick begins, a slight bend or "preloading" in the kicking leg provides good power. The pushing leg then drifts naturally backward and off the snow to counterbalance the upper body and arms as they swing forward to begin the double pole.

The skier can divide the action into two parts: 1. the "extended" phase where the arms swing forward and the kicking leg drifts back; and 2. the "contracted" phase where double poling occurs. The kick occurs between the two phases.

The kick double pole should be a natural extension of the double pole rather than an artificial lifting of the leg. Again, resist the temptation to

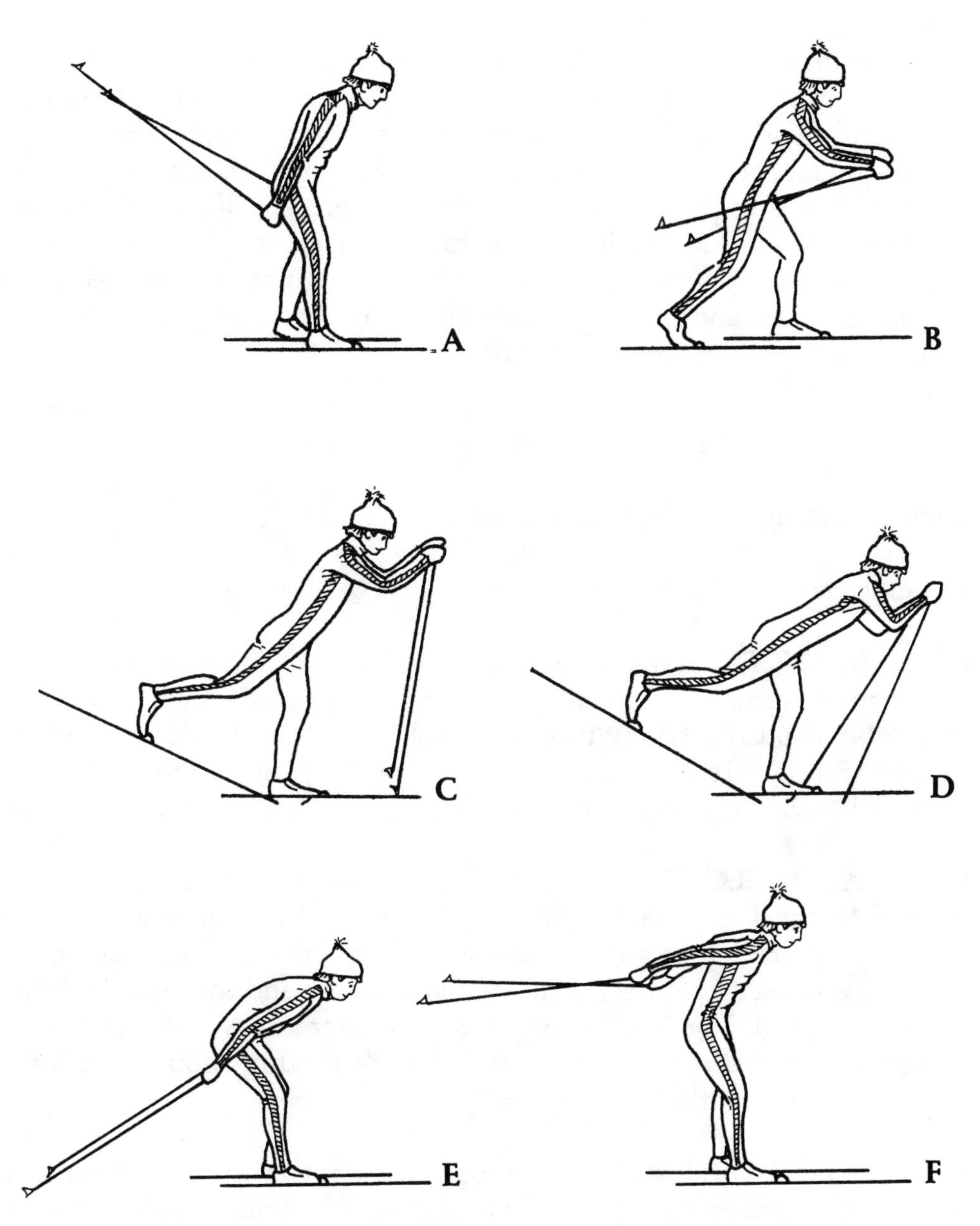

The *kick double pole* relies on strong push off (A, B) to move forward and good forward lean (C) for strong double poling (D, E, F).

strive for that perfect magazine image. Skiers who focus on the backward extension often lose their timing and kick too late when their feet are behind their hips. A subtle way to practice is to simply double pole and let the feet separate slightly as a natural counterbalance. Eventually, the skier is able to push off one foot slightly before it lifts off the snow.

Alternating the kicking leg is the most relaxed way to kick double pole. Skiers usually begin their practice by kicking with the same foot to develop good timing and then they strive to alternate legs to develop good rhythm and minimize fatigue.

Practice

Skills: Sliding, poling, pushing off.

Terrain: Flat.

BASIC STANCE. Stand on your skis as if ready to dive into a pool—with hands extended backward, bent over at the waist. Swing the arms forward and push off the "platform" with one foot. Glide forward on one ski and prepare to double-pole. After pushing against the poles, the pushing leg should drift forward and into the track next to the other ski.

OPEN AND CLOSED. This drill uses two words to establish a rhythm to the kick double pole. Say "open" when you push off and extend your arms forward to plant the poles. (The pushing foot drifts back.) Say "closed" after the double poling occurs and the arms and foot approach the gliding leg. Every time you utter the word, your body should be in the correct position. Your body's rhythm should match the cadence of the words.

LONGEST DOUBLE POLE. Establish a starting point on a track and then back up fifteen feet. Stride down the track to build speed, kick double pole at the starting point, and ride out the glide. Mark the ending point. Repeat the exercise, and try to beat your mark by lengthening glide. Experiment with deeper compression in double poling and stronger pushing off. Also try striding more slowly for a smoother transition into the kick double pole. This is an excellent exercise to practice the transition.

PARTNER PUSHES. Try this exercise with a trusting friend (without poles), standing face to face with ski tips overlapping. Assume the "extended" or "open" stance with arms forward and one leg backward. Your palms touch those of your partner to provide stability. Then simulate the double poling by swinging your extended arms and leg toward the supporting leg—the "closed" position. Swing back to the open stance again and meet your partner's palms with your own. Both people have to be synchronized to provide stability! Develop a good rhythm with the open and closed positions, then alternate the leg that moves backward. This emphasizes the timing nicely.

Problem	**Solution**
Poor timing	The kicking leg pushes against the snow too late and drags behind the body. Let the kick double pole happen naturally. Refrain from pushing off too strongly at the outset; let the kicking foot drift back slightly as a counterbalance to the upper body. Use the Open and Closed exercise to establish rhythm.
Straight leg	If the gliding leg straightens while you ride the ski, your power is heading for the sky and balance becomes a problem. Keep the leg flexed at the knee and the weight centered over the ski.
Poor double poling	See the Double Pole section.

Freestyle Cross-Country Skiing

5

Skating isn't a completely new aspect of cross-country skiing, because skiers have used skate turns and skating without poles for many years. But refinement of V-skating maneuvers in recent years has brought a new awareness of their power and speed. Now even young children in elementary school are skating along ski trails.

Mike Gallagher, former Olympian and coach of the U.S. Ski Team, reminisced recently about the early years of Nordic competition when skiers skated off the starting line to break ahead of the pack and then shifted into the diagonal stride for the duration of the race. He was laughing about skating's history during a training session with examiners from Professional Ski Instructors of America in the East.

Gallagher observed that racers didn't accept skating as the best racing technique initially, but he said the perception at the time was that it took too much strength to be effective throughout an entire race. As the conditioning of athletes improved and skating helped skiers win races, freestyle skiing finally jumped in popularity.

V-skating occurs on groomed snow without tracks, and it is used to move uphill quickly and to accelerate on flat and downhill terrain. Although skating requires more strength from the skier, the payoff is greater. It allows a skier to glide farther faster, and its exhilarating speed has proved popular with recreational skiers who have welcomed these challenging new moves.

Skating is faster than traditional moves for three reasons: 1. the skis are always moving; 2. the push-off or kick phase is stronger; and 3. the longer poles generate power for a longer period. In traditional moves, the ski actually pauses momentarily as a skier sets the wax pocket to push forward. In skating, a skier pushes off an edged ski that is still moving.

The type and timing of poling with V-skating varies greatly, but all the combinations promote more consistent power throughout the ski moves. This mixing and matching of poling and skating makes skiers more versatile and better able to handle changes in terrain.

When I learned to skate in the last decade, I realized that I had actually used these moves before, although in a more primitive form! Differences in the landscape had forced me to alter my poling, especially when skating around corners on trails, but I'd always believed my instinctive changes to be wrong because they were a departure from the currently accepted form. As you explore the various skating moves, you may experience that same feeling of familiarity. After all, they do flow naturally from other skiing maneuvers, which is the intent of this practice.

NO-POLE SKATING

Basic V-skating without poles is a fast way to move across flat terrain or down hills. It is practiced when the skier is moving so quickly that poling is unnecessary. In fact, poling would disrupt rhythm and balance.

Skating on skis is similar to skating on ice, and this familiar move makes it appealing to a variety of skiers who want to experiment with new skating moves. I enjoy the sensation of feeling like a speed skater as I skate aggressively from ski to ski.

Eliminating the poling can be initially unnerving to those who tend to use their poles as crutches, but it simply and easily introduces skiers to skating by asking them to use only their legs. Any timing problems between poling and skating are thus eliminated.

Skiers hold their skis in a V shape, tails together, and skate from leg to leg. They hold their poles loosely but securely in their hands and swing their arms naturally in an alternating fashion (as in the diagonal stride). They ride each skating ski as long as possible with the body above each foot, and this centered position lets them push off onto the new ski. Beginner skaters maintain balance by shorter gliding and by transfer-

No pole skating is an aggressive way to maintain or increase momentum on flat terrain and downhills. The skier is moving too quickly to pole effectively.

ring the weight quickly from ski to ski. As comfort increases, skiers tend to pump their arms more strongly, like a speed skater, push off firmly with a flexed knee, extend the "skating" leg fully after pushing off, and as a result glide farther along the trail.

Children especially begin to skate instinctively when they want to go fast, and edging their skis to move forward provides them with more support than the more subtle action of pushing off to diagonal-stride down the track. As skating has matured, the no-pole skate has become an aggressive means of accelerating on downhills before going low into a tuck position.

No-pole skating introduces the technical elements that you will use with every skating maneuver. Subsequent moves focus primarily upon the changes in poling. Refer to this section for a review if you have any subsequent problems with the other maneuvers.

Practice

Skills: Gliding on one ski, moving from ski to ski, pushing off, edging, poling.

Terrain: Flat, downhill.

BASIC STANCE. With skis in a V position, tails together, balance on one ski. Center the body over the ski. Then step onto the other ski and center the body again. Edge the ski as you push off it, and you'll be able to push yourself fully over the new ski.

The arms swing naturally in an alternating fashion, just like ice skating. The opposing arm points toward the skating (gliding) ski.

ROCKING Vs. In a stationary position, rock from ski to ski. Watch how the ski edges as you push off it. Each time you push off, bring the leg (and ski) over to the other for a "closed" stance. From this centered position over the ski you'll be able to step forward farther. The skis will begin to glide naturally.

TOE-KNEE-NOSE. Align the toes, knees, and nose over each ski to encourage complete weight transfer. You should be able to look straight down and see your knees over the ski. If anything is out of alignment, you'll fall off the ski—usually to the inside because you haven't committed your entire body to the gliding ski.

BODY SWIVELS. Orient the zipper on your jacket or ski suit over the skating ski. Your body will swivel or rotate so that it faces each skating ski.

CLICKING THE HEELS. Each time you skate, bring the trailing foot next to the gliding foot to stay centered over the ski. Touch the feet together at the outset to exaggerate the position. Once skating speed builds, let the trailing foot come in near the other foot before you glide onto the new ski.

SPEED SKATING. Swing the arms vigorously like a speed skater, pointing the opposite hand toward the tip of the gliding ski. This helps to propel the body forward over the gliding ski.

DRIBBLING. Dribble a ball across the snow by hitting it with your skis. This enjoyable and challenging activity promotes lots of one-ski gliding and quick changes of direction.

READING THE TRACKS. Skate across a groomed area covered by light snow and analyze your tracks. The beginning of each track should be flat and wide to show that you are riding a flattened ski. (A flat ski enhances glide because it reduces drag against the snow.) The ski is edged just before you push off onto the new ski. The end of each track should be narrower to show the edging.

SLALOM COURSE. Establish a slalom course with ski poles or markers in a straight line, and skate around the poles. At first you may have to skate several times to get around each pole. But eventually strive to skate once around each pole and lengthen your glide. Change the slalom into an offset course by moving the poles apart in a zigzag fashion. Try to skate around the poles.

Problem	Solution
Short glide	The skier feels insecure gliding on one ski and transfers weight quickly. The result is a fast tempo that uses more energy. Use the one-ski exercises in Chapter 3. The dribbling exercise is also helpful for staying relaxed.
Straddling	The skier is keeping his weight in the middle over the snow and needs to move fully onto the skating ski. Use Toe-Knee-Nose, Mary Poppins, Body Swivels, and Clicking the Heels to transfer weight completely. Straddling can give a skier more comfort because the time spent gliding on one ski is shortened. But the quick tempo is tiring.
Skidding	Skiers are stepping sideways rather than forward onto the gliding ski. A wider V shape will also encourage stronger edging. Use the Rocking Vs exercise with skis in a wide V, and edge the skis firmly.
Upright stance	More aggressive forward lean with the upper body improves a skier's balance and power. Strive to move the hips ahead of the skating foot (the one you will push off). Use the Speed Skating exercise.

MARATHON SKATE

This maneuver marks the transition from classical skiing to freestyle because it combines skating with track skiing. Its introduction signaled a major change in cross-country skiing when Bill Koch first introduced it to World Cup races. Skiers had skated around corners, but the marathon skate led the way to experimentation with new skating maneuvers for racing uphill.

The marathon skate requires tracks (unlike the new skating moves), where the skier combines double poling with an extra push from a ski angled across the track—a half-skate action. The other ski remains in the track and moves forward. The upper body adds power through double poling, while one leg simultaneously adds power through skating.

As skiers swing their arms forward to begin the double pole, they also lift one leg from the track and angle the ski across it. Their ski tails cross, but the gliding ski is deeper in the track and the skis do not touch. The feet are close together when the skis assume a half-V formation.

As the skier begins to pole, he steps forward onto the skating ski and glides on it. The skier glides on the skating ski as he continues poling behind his body. As the glide diminishes, he pushes off the skating ski onto the ski gliding in the track to continue good momentum.

An important element in the marathon skate is transferring weight from the gliding ski onto the skating ski. Effective weight transfer allows you to move your body over the skating ski and push off it strongly for forward power. This returns the body over the tracked ski so you can initiate the next double pole from a strong, stable position.

This skill is often overlooked by the beginner, who pushes off the tracked ski continually without transferring weight. But I've also watched some accomplished intermediate skiers do this, and I marvel at the strength of the leg in the track. It takes a lot of work to balance continually on one leg!

Timing is crucial for skiers to remain balanced. Otherwise, they risk splitting their skis or planting their poles between their legs; either situation causes skiers to fall forward, often abruptly. Timing is a good focus at the beginning to coordinate the maneuver.

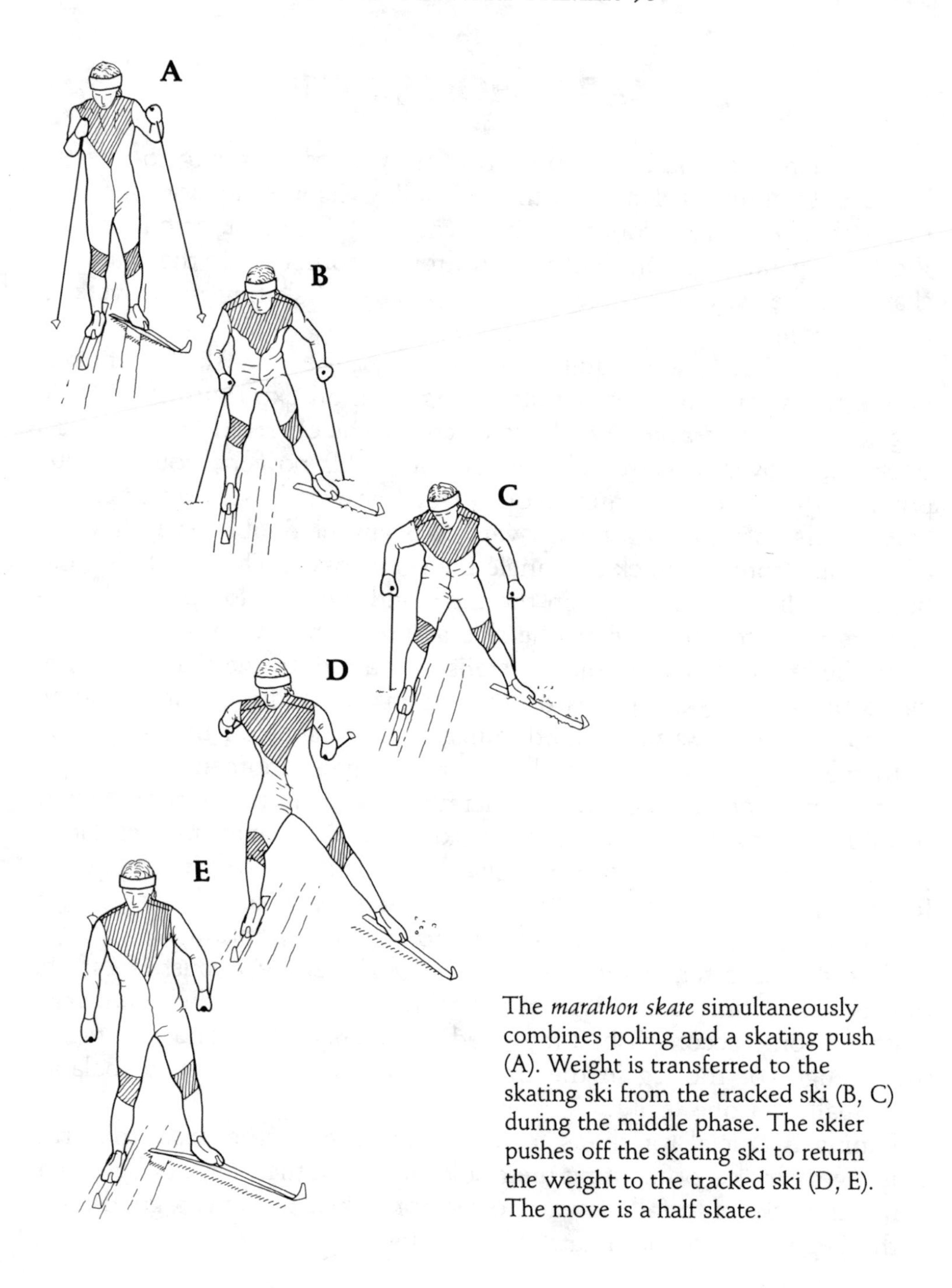

The *marathon skate* simultaneously combines poling and a skating push (A). Weight is transferred to the skating ski from the tracked ski (B, C) during the middle phase. The skier pushes off the skating ski to return the weight to the tracked ski (D, E). The move is a half skate.

Practice

Skills: Gliding on one ski, moving from ski to ski, edging, pushing off, poling.

Terrain: Flat, gentle incline.

BASIC STANCE. Balance on one ski in the tracks and angle the other ski across the track in a V, tails together. Rock back and forth from the angled ski to the track ski, transferring weight completely so you stand fully on one ski at a time. Let the tracked ski lift off the snow and click against the skating ski.

Now synchronize the poling and skating ski in a stationary exercise. Each time you step onto the angled ski, plant the poles. Keep the poling just outside and behind the skating ski to avoid inadvertently planting the poles between the legs! It's a common cause of abrupt falling.

Center your body over the skating ski as you simulate the follow-through with the poling. Then push off the skating ski and transfer weight back to the tracked ski. Centering your body over the tracked ski enables you to initiate strong double poling again and to step forward onto the skating ski.

Begin with gentle steps *forward* and short glides until the timing is solid.

SYNCHRONIZED POLE-STEP. This drill emphasizes good timing. To get moving, you sometimes pole before skating. But once you are gliding, the poling and stepping forward occur simultaneously. Use a buzzword like "step" or "pole" to coordinate the actions.

ROCKING Vs. In a stationary V position, practice good weight transfer by rocking from ski to ski. Let the tracked ski lift from the track until it clicks against the angled ski.

Begin the marathon skate, and let the track ski lift slightly every time you glide onto the skating ski. This reminds you to transfer weight completely.

MARY POPPINS. Check that your starting position is "closed" and balanced. Skis rest in a half-V with the legs together, knees and ankles next to each other. Avoid bending the knees excessively and lifting the skating foot to present a bowlegged appearance. Perform the marathon skate and make sure the legs come back together each time.

SCOOTERS (WITHOUT POLES). Use the skating ski to push down the track. Transfer weight from the tracked to the skating ski for a better push.

VARIABLE Vs. Change the shape of the V to get moving (wider) and to maintain speed (narrower).

SKI LIFTS. Each time you glide onto the skating ski, lift the tracked ski slightly. This action encourages weight transfer. Then dampen this effect so the tracked ski remains on the snow.

TOE-KNEE-NOSE. Keep the toe, knee, and nose aligned over each ski to promote good weight transfer. If the body fails to align over the ski, then you rush the weight transfer, increase the tempo, and shorten glide. This alignment forces the body to move back and forth over each ski, and the body actually points out over the skating ski. The head almost follows a circular path because of compression combined with the weight shift.

Keeping the leg in the track relatively straight is helpful and eliminates fatigue. Any excessive bending of either leg is too taxing and generates little extra power.

THE FORWARD STEP. Step forward onto the skating ski to stay centered over it and skate powerfully. Stepping sideways sends the momentum that way and causes the foot and ski to get left behind. The body begins to move backward also. Weak glide results.

THE FORWARD SLIDE. Smooth the forward step into a *slide* forward. This eliminates any step downward that sends the force into the snow. The forward slide encourages all power to be transferred into good glide on the skating ski.

BOWING. Use strong upper-body compressions to increase power in the double poling and lengthen glide. If the skating is strong, you may not need compressions that are as deep as pure double poling.

SWITCHING LEGS. Once you have practiced the marathon skate with each leg, begin to alternate the skating legs to minimize fatigue. Marathon-skate along the track with one leg for a short distance, then perform a pure double pole with both skis in the track, then switch to skating with the other leg. This exercise assumes that you have practice tracks without adjacent snow banks that interfere with skating.

SWITCHING TRACKS. Once you feel comfortable with riding the gliding ski, begin to switch tracks. Ride the gliding ski across the trail to a new set of tracks, double-pole in the tracks, then begin the marathon skate with the new skating leg.

Problem	**Solution**
Lack of timing	The poling and skating does not occur simultaneously for a coordinated burst of power. Use the Synchronized Pole-Step drills to recapture the timing.
Lack of compression	Learning to use the legs properly tends to interfere with good compression. Refocus on double poling with Bowing exercises and push the poles past the body for good follow-through. This increases the power from double poling. Refer to the Double

	Poling section in Chapter 4 for more exercises.
No weight transfer	Keeping the weight on the tracked ski prevents you from moving onto the skating ski. The skating leg pushes weakly and generates little power to keep you moving forward. The body tends to move backward as a result, and squatting can result. Use Rocking Vs, Ski Lifts, and Toe-Knee-Nose to promote good weight transfer.

V1 SKATE

V1 is the first of the skating moves where the skis function in a full-V position. When skiers approach a steeper hill, more power is needed to continue their momentum. The legs alone cannot provide enough power to handle a steep ascent, and poling becomes necessary. V1 skating is often the favored move because it allows skiers to shift smoothly and continue climbing uphill.

V1 is skating with double poling on one side only; for every two skating steps, the skier double-poles once. The timing remains the same as the marathon skate; skiers step and pole simultaneously. After poling, they ride the gliding ski—the "power side"—and push off onto the other ski as they follow through with their poling. This ski is sometimes referred to as the "free glide side" because no poling occurs over it.

Skiers face each ski as they glide on it and also angle their poles over the ski. They pole over the gliding ski, shift their poles over the free-glide ski, and then swing them back to the gliding ski to begin double poling again. The arms and head appear to travel in a circular motion as the skier bends over and rises through the compression.

Skiers do not intentionally use a syncopated or staggered pole-plant to obtain more power. Although I sometimes use the staggered plant to get

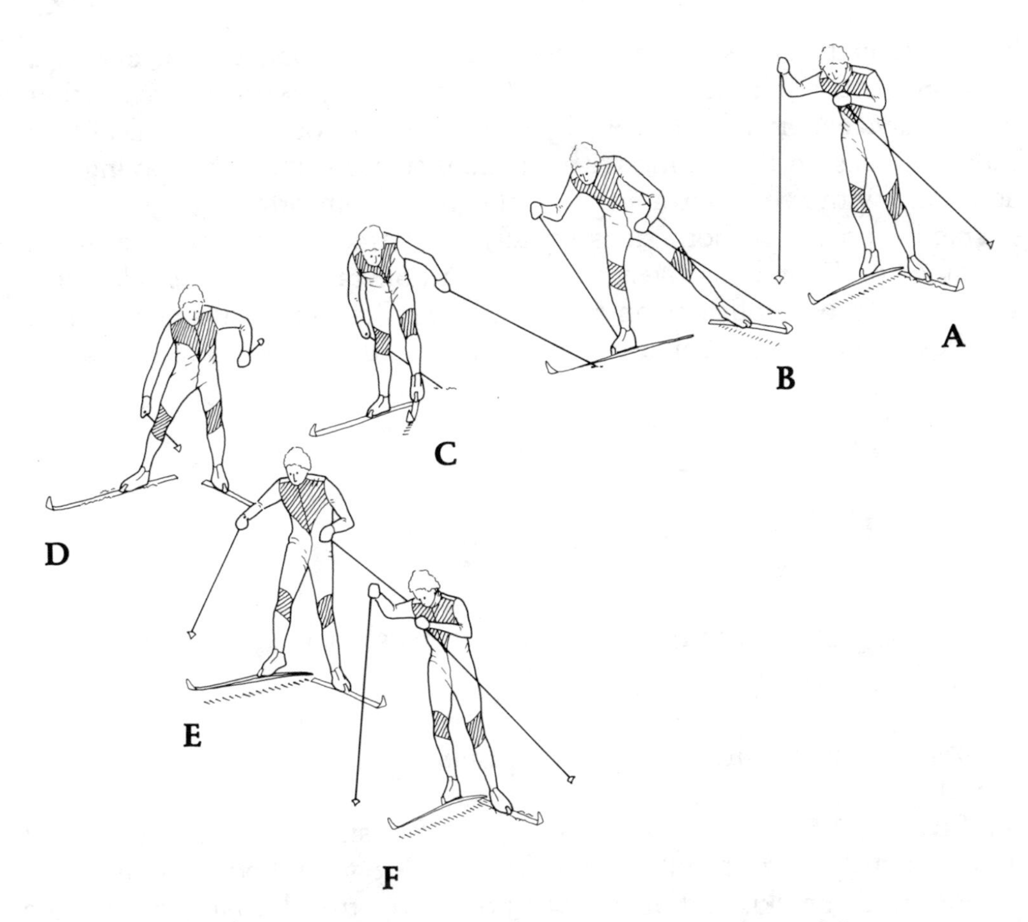

V1 skating is similar to the marathon skate except it uses a full skate out of the tracks. The skier aligns his body over the poling ski (A, B), prepares to skate onto the new ski (C), transfers his weight (D), and prepares to return to the poling side (E, F).

moving, I plant both poles simultaneously when I'm under way. The pole positioning is offset or asymmetical, with one hand higher than the other. The skier appears to "hang" off the higher hand before pushing against the poles.

A variety of exercises is useful in learning V1. Some find it easier to begin without skis when gliding undermines balance. This approach allows a skier to focus on an efficient stance and good timing first and develop good habits more quickly than struggling with gliding. Other people have experienced success by beginning without poles. This allows them to focus on the timing without the increased speed that poling can add. Play with whatever approach feels most comfortable to you.

Practice poling on both sides equally. I favored my strong side when learning to V1 and discovered in a marathon race that it would have been nice to be proficient on the other side. Practicing in a race wasn't the best environment for learning with limited frustration, and it's not recommended!

Practice

Skills: Gliding on one ski, moving from ski to ski, edging, poling, pushing off.

Terrain: Flat terrain and gentle uphills.

BASIC STANCE. Stand with skis in a V position, tails together, and poles angled forward with hands in front of your body. Swing your hands over one ski, and align your body over the ski. Notice how the hands appear to be offset—the outside hand is higher, and the inside hand is lower. You almost hang off the high hand with your forearm close to the pole. From this position, the double poling begins.

Start from the forward position again, close your eyes, and move into the basic stance over your poling side. Check to make sure your hands frame the skis and your body rotates around to align itself over the ski.

STEP-AND-POLE (WITH POLES, WITHOUT SKIS). Take off the skis and focus on this timing drill without worrying about balancing on skis. Choose one side to be your poling or power side. Step and pole at the same time on this side, then step onto the other foot without poling. Swing the poles back to the power side. Repeat these actions to develop a good rhythm, making sure that your poles and foot strike the ground simultaneously.

Then begin to step forward slightly, again concentrating on the coordinated stepping and poling. The next step is framing each ski with your arms, poling on one side, and recovering the poles along the other ski.

Change your poling side and repeat these steps. If one side feels more comfortable, you may want to practice the exercises on that side first. But switch to the other side eventually to develop it equally or you may become dependent on one side.

STEP-AND-POLE (WITH SKIS, WITHOUT POLES). Imitate the poling motions and coordinate them with the stepping onto the skis. Swing the arms naturally and completely behind the body during the poling phase. As you recover over the free-glide side, swing the arms forward in line with the skis and let them lead the rest of your body in rising over the skis. This helps to center your body. Remember to compress the torso for a longer, stronger poling phase.

STEP-AND-POLE (WITH SKIS AND POLES). Emphasize the simultaneous stepping and poling in place first. Plant the poles outside the skis, and push gently. (Little follow-through with the poling will occur because you will be barely moving.) Then take small steps forward and walk down the track. Once the timing is solid, begin to push off more strongly and slide the skis across the snow. As you glide farther, the poling extends farther behind your body.

ONE-POLE V1. Use the one pole in your "tall" hand as you prepare to V1. You can "hang" off this pole as you plant with the forearm near the pole. Push through strongly and extend the pole behind your body. This helps to rotate your torso toward the other ski to help step onto it.

POLE CHANT. With increased speed, the timing may falter. Use a key word like "pole" on your power side to step and pole simultaneously. The rhythm becomes "pole"—pause—"pole"—pause as you skate between the power ski and the free-glide ski. Ski smooth rather than fast.

SLIDE-AND-POLE. Push each ski across the snow when you move onto it. Rather than stomping onto the ski (and sending your momentum into the ground), imagine scuffing bubble gum off its bottom and sliding it forward (to send your energy in that direction).

MARY POPPINS. Keep your legs relatively straight and close together before skating onto each ski. This centers the body over the ski so that you can ride a flat ski longer. Failing to bring the legs together encourages straddling with your weight between the skis and develops short, choppy glide as you rock between the skis.

AROUND THE WORLD. Focus on the path of your arms. They should frame the skis and travel in a triangular "around-the-world" path. Poling occurs downward over the power side and pole recovery occurs upward over the free-glide side with a quick transition back to the power side. The body rotates and faces one ski, then the other, as it also travels around the world.

APE SKATING. Let your arms swing low past your knees as you pole. Compressing the upper body is necessary to reach this position. Swing the poles loosely past your body.

HIP LAUNCHES. Push off the power side and launch yourself onto the free-glide side. Get a longer glide by lifting the hips slightly and moving them ahead of your foot. As the hips lift, the torso also rises and aids in a forward projection of the body.

Now try this move gently, and think of soaring upward and forward over the free-glide ski. It moves you into an upright, forward position in preparation for double poling on the other side.

Problem	**Solution**
Poor timing	The poling and stepping onto the power side are uncoordinated. A skier with lim-

	ited one-ski balance may step too early onto the ski. Use the one-ski exercises in Chapter 3 as well as the Step-and-Pole and Pole Chant exercises here.
No or little compression	The stance is either consistently upright or hunched over, where the torso provides little power. Take a break from V1 and double-pole across the snow to regain good form. Bend over deeply, pole behind the body, and raise the torso completely. Double-pole to the base of a gentle hill and change to V1, maintaining good compression. Practice the Ape Skating drill also.
Straddling	Weight remains between the skis rather than moving completely over each ski. The skier tends to rock quickly between strongly edged skis, which diminishes glide. Emphasize the Mary Poppins foot position to tighten the stance between skating moves and use Around-the-World to get the body centered over each ski.
Inefficient double poling	See the Double Pole section in Chapter 4. Returning to pure double poling can be a relaxing break if V1 practice becomes too mechanical.

DIAGONAL V

Once the hill steepens and V1 becomes too sluggish, skiers risk losing their momentum and stalling. They can downshift into diagonal V to

The *diagonal V skate* is an aggressive extension of the gliding herringbone and allows a skier to skate up steeper hills.

keep moving up the hill. Less energy-intensive than V1, the diagonal V is an aggressive relative of the gliding herringbone.

The maneuver combines V-skating with an alternate poling motion similar to the diagonal stride. Skiers glide up the hill moving from ski to ski as they push on one pole at a time. An important element in a dynamic diagonal V is moving forward up the hill rather than rocking from side to side. The extent of the forward step depends upon the steepness of the hill; it will get shorter as the hill steepens.

Because skiers move so quickly with diagonal V, the timing of the poling varies between skiers. Some use a clear diagonal rhythm (opposite arm-and-leg pushing), but others seem to move toward a *passgang* rhythm (same-leg and same-arm pushing). This shift tends to occur with a change in the contours of the hill.

Concentrating on poling is confusing for those who are learning the diagonal V. A better focus is the dynamics of the skating action and its similarity to the gliding herringbone. Then the poling will happen naturally without affecting the power of the skating.

Skiing behind another skier is an effective way to learn the diagonal V. This imitation encourages a strong cadence with skiers moving strongly up the hill. Loosening the hips and letting them sashay over each ski does wonders for momentum. It's slightly suggestive but certainly a lot of fun, especially when practiced in pairs!

Practice

Skills: Gliding on one ski, moving from ski to ski, edging, pushing off, poling.

Terrain: Uphills.

BASIC STANCE. Stand at the base of a moderate uphill, begin to herringbone, and gradually add a few extra inches of glide. Think of pushing the ski tips just a little farther with each step. Watching the top of the hill eliminates excessive hunching over and readies the hips to move forward rather than hang back. Next time, begin to glide more aggressively at the bottom of the hill and try to carry the momentum through the steeper section.

HIP ROTATION. Move the hips strongly over the skating ski to help center the body. This promotes aggressive weight transfer. The hip rotates and provides added thrust to slide the ski farther. The sensation is like moving your hip around to bump someone. The hips sashay back and forth as you step up the hill. Exaggerate the action briefly; if you remain balanced, the rotation is still sound. The hips need to be over the skating foot in order to push off.

LITTLE STEPS, BIG STEPS. Take little steps *up* the hill, and notice how many you need to climb to the top. Gradually increase the size of the forward step, moving forward rather than to the side—the number of required steps will decrease. But giant steps inhibit your ability to push off the lower ski, so don't take too big a step.

Problem	**Solution**
Stepping on ski tails	Step forward up the hill so the skis move free of each other. Stepping to the side causes the tails to click together and limits forward motion.
Blocked hips	Stiff hips inhibit good glide. Move to a gentler hill and use the Hip Rotation exercise to loosen the hips. Watch the top of the hill to keep the hips tucked in and ready to move forward.
Poor timing	Don't think about the poling! Return to a herringbone on a gentler hill and then change to a gliding herringbone. Let the

power come from the legs first. Ski behind a good skier and match the cadence.

V2 SKATE

V2 skating is a powerful move that enhances gliding, but skiers need good balance to learn it without frustration. The maneuver generally is used to accelerate on flat terrain or down hills, where the sensation of flying on skis is exhilarating. Strong skiers can also use it to climb easy and moderate hills if they carry their momentum from flat terrain.

Skiers double-pole over each skating ski in V2; for every two skating steps, double poling occurs twice. A change in the timing becomes important to provide more consistent power and stability through the move. The double poling is not synchronized with the skating steps. The poling occurs after the skier glides on the ski and prior to the push-off.

Being able to glide on one ski is essential for learning V2. Skiers use good forward body lean with the hips high and forward of the feet. Then they pole over the ski, and as their hands near their legs they shift their weight to the other ski. The toe-knee-nose rule applies and the body must be firmly centered over the new gliding ski. They complete the poling, bring their feet together, and prepare to pole again.

V2 is a symmetrical move in that the same actions occur for each ski. The angle of the skis is usually smaller because the skier is traveling quickly. The greatest difficulty at the beginning is handling the speed, and I've suffered some spectacular high-speed crashes as a result of feeling invincible with V2. The sensation of soaring on skis is tremendous, until the rocky landing reminds us that flying is meant for those with wings. Alpine skiers will find the move familiar because they also use it to gain speed on flat terrain or at the start of a race course.

Practice

Skills: Gliding on one ski, moving from ski to ski, edging,

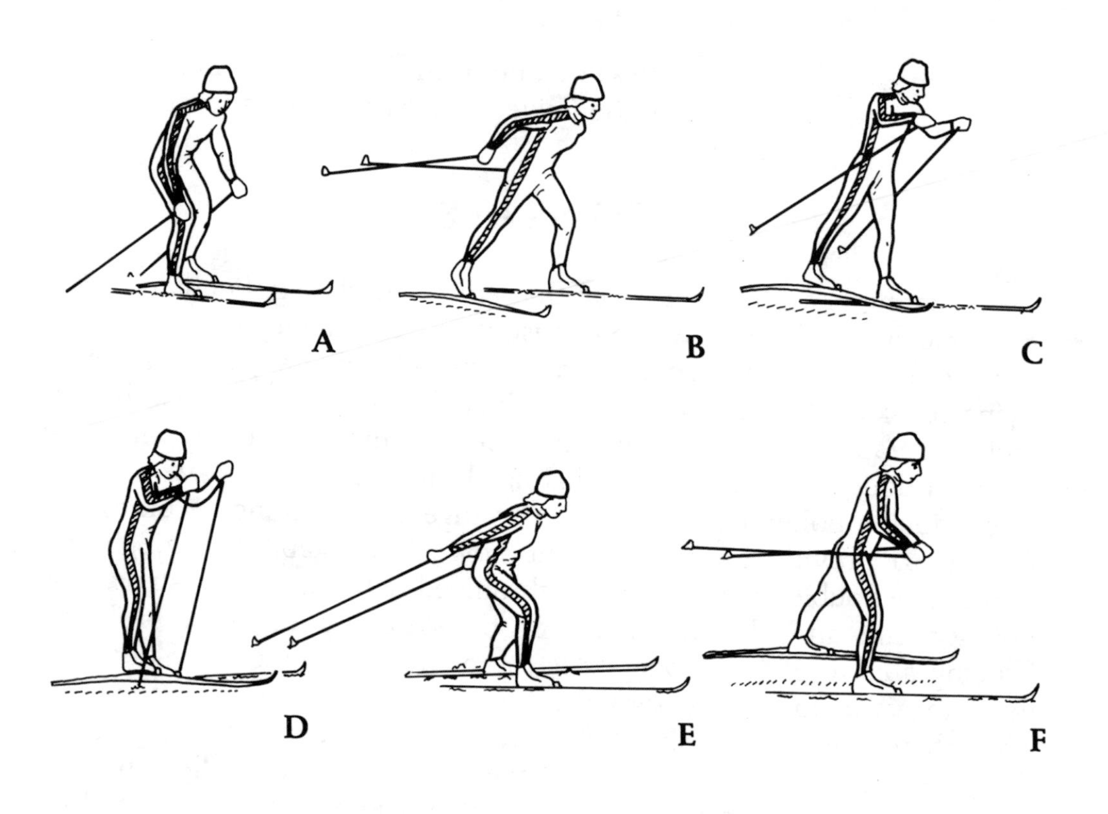

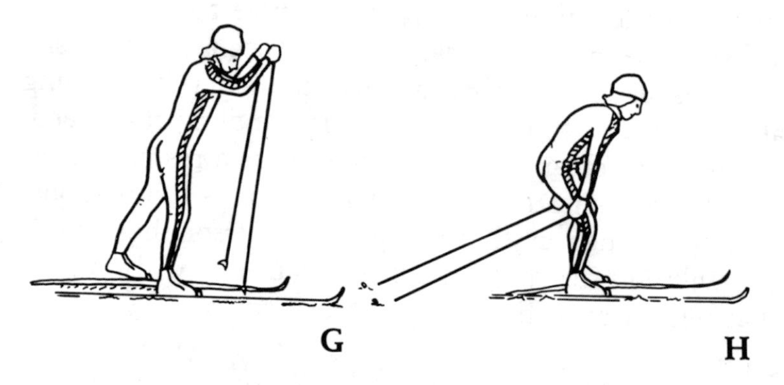

Double poling occurs with every skate in V2 skating. As his hands approach his body (A), the skier skates onto the new gliding ski (B). He prepares to double pole over the ski (C, D), shifts weight to the new ski, and follows through with the poling (E). The skier prepares to double pole over the new ski (F, G, H) to continue skating.

pushing off, poling.

Terrain: Flat, downhill, easy-to-moderate uphill.

BASIC STANCE. Practice the timing of poling and stepping in a stationary position first. Hold the poles at their midlengths. Step onto one ski and mimic the double poling over the ski. As your hands approach your body, step onto the other ski, placing it in a V-shaped position. Move your hands over the skis and begin to pole again. Step onto the other ski as your hands approach your body.

STEP-AND-POLE. Continue to hold the poles at their midlengths. Step forward onto one ski and double-pole. As the hands approach the body, step forward onto the other ski. Continue stepping forward until the timing feels secure. Some gliding may occur naturally, but the primary focus here is good timing.

TWO-SKI GLIDE. This exercise simulates the pattern of V2 movement, but gliding occurs securely on two skis. Glide onto one ski and bring the second ski parallel to it. Double-pole over the skis. As the hands approach the body, step diagonally in the other direction and bring the other ski parallel. Double-pole over the skis. Practice this down the trail until the step-and-pole timing is solid.

Eventually glide onto just one ski, and bring the other ski over without standing on it. Double-pole and glide onto the new leg. That's V2! If you become wobbly, just set the other ski on the snow to regain your balance. Revert to the two-ski glide to maintain your balance and rhythm before you switch to one ski again.

POWER POLING. Use the Two-Ski Glide exercise to concentrate on the double poling. Extend the poling behind the body as you step in the new direction. Glide on the skis while you complete the poling. Then recover the poles over your skis and double-pole. Repeat the sequence, using good compression to extend the poling behind your body. Let your hands meet behind your back for a while. Be relaxed and enjoy the ride on the gliding skis.

Then change to a pure V2, gliding on one ski, while you continue good follow-through with the poling.

GLIDE-AND-POLE. Use this chant to reinforce the timing with V2. Think "glide-and-pole" to stagger the timing. The "and" becomes an important waiting phase to complete the pole recovery over the gliding ski and delay the pole-plant. Novices often want to pole and skate simultaneously. Momentary loss of balance tends to interfere with good timing, and skiers want to pole too soon to increase their security.

The chant can be handy to regain timing while you are still moving. Hold off on the poling, but continue to skate. Then reintroduce the poling to the tune of the chant.

POLE-AND-SKATE. This exercise is the same as the one above, but it gives you a new way to think about the timing. The same guideline applies: As your hands approach your leg during poling, skate onto the new gliding ski.

LEANING TOWER. With each poling recovery over the gliding ski, lift your torso into a forward "leaning tower" over the ski. The arms follow quickly and lift upward to continue this forward momentum. Your weight hurtles forward and leads into crisp, powerful double poling. (Otherwise, you plant your face!) Sometimes the unweighted foot hangs behind the supporting foot as a comfortable counterbalance.

POWER PUSH-OFFS. Spring diagonally forward off the edged ski to move onto the new ski. Point your toes as you push off and bring the toes near the new gliding foot. Think "toe-off" each time you push off.

Problem	Solution
Poor balance	Use the Two-Ski Glide concept at any point in the V2 to regain balance. Gradu-

	ally decrease the amount of time spent on two skis.
Timing	Speed can undermine the timing of skating and poling; skiers almost move too quickly to be able to double-pole and stay balanced. Use the Step-and-Pole exercise from a stationary position. Then continue the emphasis with the Glide-and-Pole chant.
Poor double poling	Target each problem area in double poling—lack of compression, arm collapse, lack of arm extension—and refer to the corrective exercises in that section in Chapter 4.

V2 ALTERNATE

V2 alternate is another means of accelerating across flat terrain, and it is identical to V2 except for the poling. This move helps skiers to retain their balance while moving quickly; too much poling would disrupt rhythm and speed. V2 alternate is one of the fastest moves on flat and undulating terrain.

Double poling occurs once for every two skating steps (like V1), but the timing of the poling and skating is just like V2. The skier glides on one ski, double-poles over that ski (power side), glides onto the other ski (free-glide side), refrains from poling, glides onto the other ski, and double-poles again.

This hybrid of V1 and V2 has earned itself many names in its evolution—among others, V1 off-timing and the Gunde skate, because Swedish National Team skier Gunde Svan showed its effectiveness early in World Cup races. V2 alternate has become the accepted term in an effort to eliminate confusion.

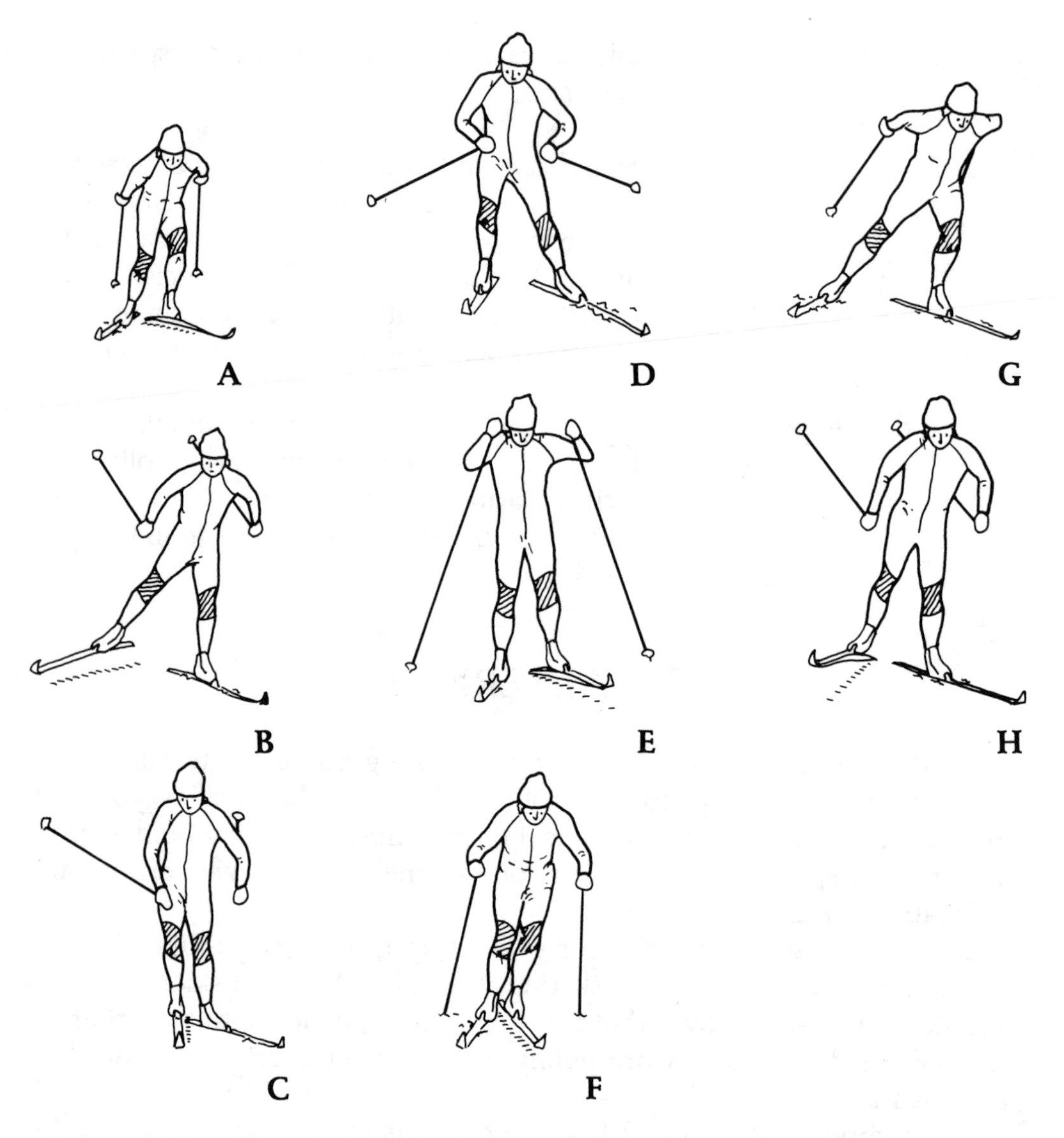

V2 alternate is similar to V2, but the skier poles on only one side. The skier skates onto a new ski (A), and glides on it (B). He returns the arms to a plant position for double poling (C, D, E,) and double poles. As his hands approach his body (F), he glides onto the other ski (G) and prepares to repeat the sequence (H).

Once skiers discover the V2 alternate timing, they realize the versatility of all the poling rhythms in skating. They begin to experiment with the poling and to combine various moves easily. Sliding from no-pole skating to V2 alternate and V2 becomes natural at high speeds to handle changes in terrain.

V2 alternate was the last skating move I learned, and once I perfected the timing I realized I had used the maneuver a few years earlier without knowing it. It happened during the season when I started to experiment with V1 skating and I thought I was blowing the timing of the poling. I worked painstakingly that year to eliminate the "error"; it was V2 alternate that I eliminated.

Practice

Skills: Gliding on one ski, moving from ski to ski, edging, pushing off, poling.

Terrain: Flat or undulating terrain.

BASIC STANCE. Practice the timing in a stationary position, holding the poles at their midlengths. Step onto one ski and mimic the double poling. As the hands approach the body, step onto the other ski. Keep the hands behind the body and step back onto the first ski. Double-pole again and repeat the sequence. A good timing device to get going is the chant of "step, pole, step, step, pole."

STEP-POLE. Holding the poles at their midlengths, repeat the exercise but step forward as you chant.

GLIDE-POLE. Holding the poles normally, change the above stepping exercise into a gliding one.

HAND TOUCHES. Double-pole with good compression and extend the arms completely behind the body. Touch the hands together to test your rearward arm extension.

Problem	Solution
Poor timing	Begin from a stationary stance and use the Step-Pole exercise to recapture the timing. Excessive speed can tempt you to rush the poling, so take small steps. Then continue to the Glide-Pole Drill.
Poor poling	Follow through completely behind the body with the poles rather than shortening the poling phase. The arms are moving at a slower speed than the legs, but the tendency is to rush the pole-recovery phase. Let them swing slowly back to the power side.

Cross-Country Downhill Skiing

6

The rediscovery of the telemark turn has created a new sport that is an exciting hybrid of Nordic and alpine skiing. Cross-country downhill blurs the distinction between the two skiing worlds and promotes a better understanding of each one. Is it more alpine or Nordic? Who cares about such distinctions . . . it's first-class skiing.

Free heels give skiers the flexibility to dip their knees into the telemark turn as they swoop downhill. But to call them "telemark" skiers is limiting, because they mix cross-country moves like the telemark turn with alpine moves like the parallel turn. A telemark skier can do everything that an alpine skier can—plus one more turn!

I watched a group of telemark skiers descend a Vermont trail during the first certification exam in the East for telemark instructors with Tony Forrest, the coach of the National Demonstration Team for Professional Ski Instructors of America. He urged me to block my view of the skiers' lower legs with my hand and watch them just from the knees up. They looked just like alpine skiers and used the same skiing dynamics. The only difference was that the Nordic downhill skiers slid their feet into different positions.

Good balance is an important skill in cross-country downhill skiing because the binding prevents the skier from leaning back or forward excessively against his or her boots. The sure-footed stance of accomplished cross-country downhill skiers lets them handle the same terrain as do alpine skiers.

This chapter introduces a progression of downhill moves to practice on telemark equipment. The maneuvers range from the beginner level to advanced moves suitable for steep terrain. However, all cross-country skiers use these downhill moves, and the exercises are also suitable for skiers on touring equipment.

The practice terrain for the exercises is generally flat and gentle downhills, but all exercises can be repeated on steeper terrain as skiers develop the ability to handle more difficult hills.

STRAIGHT RUN

This introductory move orients skiers to the hill and helps them to develop good balance when sliding. Sliding straight downhill is a simple move that develops good habits and makes subsequent maneuvers proceed more smoothly. Because balance and comfort are the priorities, the best practice takes place on a gentle downhill slope with a flat landing zone that lets skiers coast to a stop. Learning to stop comes later in the practice.

Skiers adopt the "All-Purpose Sports Stance" introduced in the sliding exercises in Chapter 3. They "slump" into position with bent ankles and knees, a quiet torso, and hands low and in front of the thighs. The initial focus is sliding with a relaxed body that absorbs the bumps and dips in the hill.

The legs do the work, functioning like shock absorbers to handle the

Flexed legs and an upright torso promote good balance while sliding. A skier edges his skis to prevent slipping during a traverse of a hill.

terrain. While skiers stand with their skis parallel and their feet side by side, the legs also function independently to promote good balance. One leg often bends more than the other to maintain balance when terrain changes demand it.

Telemark wizard Dick Hall of the North American Telemark Organization calls this relaxed stance the "bag of bones" approach to skiing. He encourages skiers to stiffen up like tin soldiers, then relax their muscles until their bones support their weight. Using the skeletal structure for support provides skiers with a restful stance from which to perform all downhill moves. Skiers who shift from a tall rigid stance to a lower relaxed one will lower their center of balance and increase their stability.

Hall has sometimes unorthodox ways of encouraging skiers' comfort. I watched him lead a group through an endless series of straight-run exercises, each one with a different focus and a crazy purpose. By the end, the weakest skiers were flying off a small jump—landing on their skis at least fifty percent of the time and laughing throughout the entire experience! At the beginning, they wouldn't have considered letting their skis leave the snow. But in the end they were ready to try anything.

Practice

Skills: Sliding, gliding on one leg, moving from ski to ski, edging.

Terrain: Gentle hill.

BASIC STANCE. Stand flat-footed on the skis with feet side by side. The skis should be parallel in a wide stance beneath the line of your shoulders. Skis that are tight together provide a limited base of support. Rock from side to side to test the security of the wide stance.

Then rock forward and backward, subtly shifting your weight between the toes and heels without lifting the heels off the skis. Let the weight settle naturally between the toes and heels.

SLUMP-O-MATIC. Stand on parallel skis with the feet side by side. Stiffen the body, like a soldier, then slump into a relaxed position over the skis. Bend at the knees *and ankles* to flex the legs. Slump down the hill, letting the loose legs rise and fall like shock absorbers.

TEENAGE SLOUCH. Slide down the hill in the slouched position of an adolescent with a rounded pelvis and a slight forward lean of the torso.

QUIET HANDS. Rest your hands on your legs as you slide. Increase the bend in your legs and lean forward slightly to get your hands in position. Avoid too much forward lean, where a crouch results. Then rest your hands on your hips.

TALLER, SHORTER. Stand tall on the skis, then lower your stance by bending the legs. The lower stance provides better balance with a lowered center of gravity. Smooth the transition from the taller to shorter stance to soften jerky motions.

ANKLE ANGLES. Stand upright on the skis so your legs form a ninety-degree angle to the skis. Bend your ankles to decrease the angle between shins and skis. Experiment with different angles. An angle near forty-five degrees flexes the ankles greatly and promotes stability. However, too much flex can be tiring. Vary the angle in a straight run and find a comfortable range.

LIGHT AND LIVELY SKIS. Rock from ski to ski as you slide, letting one ski press the snow lightly. Most of your weight moves to the other ski, where you balance on a bent leg.

STRIDING AND GLIDING. "Stride" down the hill, letting one ski slide forward and then the other. Let the arms swing naturally with the stride.

ONE-LEGGED GLIDING. Glide on one ski, lifting the other ski gently off the snow. Slide on two skis to recapture your balance, then glide on the other leg. If balance is wobbly, lift only the ski tip and let the tail stay on the snow as a rudder. Balance may be better on one side if you have a stronger leg. In the future, start and finish with the weaker leg to give it extra practice.

STEP-AWAYS. Slide downhill and take a quick step to one side. Now you'll continue along a new path down the hill. A tiny step at first maintains good balance; increase the size of the sideways step as you feel more comfortable. Repeat and step to the other side.

STEP-OVERS. Step sideways over an obstacle like a hat or mitten. The obstacle forces you to lift the foot a little higher as you step. Repeat and step the other way.

TRAVERSES. On a steeper hill, slide across the hill in a traverse. Edge the skis into the hill to prevent skidding out. Your knees point into the hill while your upper body faces the direction of glide. (As the hill steepens, the torso begins to rotate around farther and face down the fall line. Your knees point more strongly into the hill.) Gradually point the tips more downhill as you become comfortable with the speed. Your weight should be evenly distributed between both skis on the traverse.

ONE-LEGGED TRAVERSES. Experiment with gliding on the downhill leg first. The inside edge of the ski digs into the snow to prevent skidding out. Then continue the traverse in the same direction and glide on the uphill leg. The outside edge of the ski digs into the snow. Return to sliding on both skis whenever you need to regain balance. Repeat with a traverse in the opposite direction.

Problem	**Solution**
Skittering skis	Relax the stiffened legs, bending at the knees and ankles in a good Slump-o-matic stance. Use Taller, Shorter and Ankle Angles to encourage flexible legs that can react smoothly to changes in terrain.
Hinging	Bending over at the waist encourages falling forward. Lift the torso upright so that it rides quietly over the legs. A little forward rounding of the shoulders, as in the Teen-

	age Slouch, helps good balance.
Sitting back	Resting too much on the heels encourages falling backward. Stand flat-footed on the skis and feel your weight settle between the toes and heels. The weight shifts slightly toward the heels when sliding downhill, but too much sends the hips backward and undermines good balance.

WEDGE (Snowplow)

The wedge or snowplow is the most basic downhill move, and it's the first tool that a beginner uses to handle descents. The familiar wedge or plow shape enables skiers to control and stop their speed. It is a useful move from which other downhill maneuvers can be initiated.

Skiers steer their skis into an A shape, with the tips almost together and the tails apart. Their torsos remain upright, while the legs bend at the ankles and knees to center their bodies over the skis. Their weight is evenly distributed between the skis.

A *gliding wedge* lets the skis slide across the snow in the A shape. Skiers stand taller, with their skis in a narrower A, and they ride out the speed of the hill. The ski stays flatter to the snow with less edging.

A *braking wedge* digs the ski edges into the snow and inhibits the skidding of the skis. It slows skiers and can bring them to a complete stop. As skiers push their skis into a wider A, they drop lower and edge the skis more.

The basic wedge can be modified into a half-wedge in groomed tracks. The skier lifts one ski from the tracks and angles it toward the tracked ski in a half-plow. The slower the skier needs to go, the lower he drops to dig the edge into the snow.

A good practice area is a gentle slope with a clear run-out to allow skiers to snowplow without worrying about stopping. As skiers can steer their skis with more control, then they can experiment with stopping farther up the hill. Skiers who tilt their torsos, wave their arms, and stiffen their legs need a gentler hill to reduce tension and concentrate on a good basic stance. Remember: When in doubt, "go low." Or as a sixth-grader yelled to a friend when reinterpreting my advice: "Go way low."

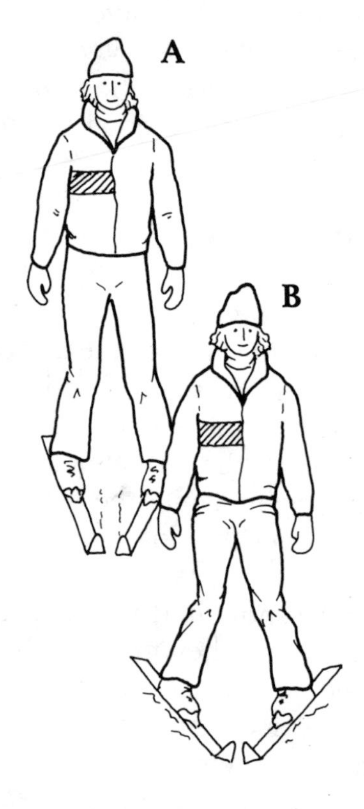

A skier stands taller in a *gliding wedge* (A) which creates a narrower wedge and greater speed. Bending the legs and widening the wedge sets the skis on edge in a *braking wedge* (B) and slows the skier's speed.

Practice

Skills: Sliding, steering, skidding, edging.

Terrain: Flat.

BASIC STANCE. Stand on parallel skis and step with one ski to form an A, tips together. Then step back to a parallel stance. Step to the other side into an A. Keep the tips separated slightly when you step into the A.

Now bend your knees and ankles when you settle into the A. Your shins press against the boot tongues if the ankles are flexed properly. Your feet appear pigeon-toed while your knees drop down over the skis. Avoid bringing the knees together into a knock-kneed stance, because it edges the skis excessively. Try it with your eyes closed, and keep a space between your knees, as if they are pressing an imaginary basketball.

Settle low in the A, rock back and forth between the skis, and settle your weight in the middle. Stay loose, flexible, relaxed. The inside of each foot should feel equal pressure along its length.

BRUSHES. Rather than stepping into position, brush one ski across the snow into the A. Brush with the other ski. Now, from a parallel position move your skis into the A simultaneously. Bend your legs and steer the ski tips together by rotating your feet. Pressing the skis apart when sinking will help.

TANDEM WEDGES. Ask a friend to push you across the snow while you are resting in a snowplow position. The friend (without skis) pushes you forward at the hips. Pushing higher tends to bend the torso over.

Then begin with the skis in a parallel position when the friend pushes you across the snow. Steer the skis into the A by rotating your feet inward. Experiment with edging the skis gently to stop the speed; push out with the heels to move the skis farther apart and help the ski edges bite the snow. This exercise helps you to become comfortable with gliding and braking wedges before you head to the hill.

Terrain: Gentle hill.

GLIDING-TO-BRAKING WEDGE. Slide downhill in a wedge and ride out the momentum until you coast to a stop. On the next run, drop gradually into a wider A when you reach flat terrain and your speed begins to subside. This edges the skis to apply the brakes and stop.

GO LOW AND SLOW. Control your speed from the top of the hill with a braking wedge, dropping lower to edge the skis. Eventually try to creep down the hill.

CHAIR SITTING. Ski in a wedge as if you are sitting on the edge of a chair with good posture. Your torso remains upright instead of bent at the waist.

SIGHTSEEING. Focus on a landmark in the distance and watch it—not your skis—as you descend.

Terrain: Moderate hill.

BRAKING-TO-GLIDING WEDGE. Ski in a braking wedge from the top to control your speed initially. Rise up gradually and narrow the wedge. This flattens the ski to increase your speed.

GO HIGH AND FLY. When you feel comfortable with a braking wedge, stand taller and flatten the skis into a gliding wedge.

TALLER, SMALLER. Stand tall in a narrower A, then drop lower into a wider A. Raise and lower your body as you descend to change the shape of your wedges.

COUNTDOWN. Use a 1 to 5 number system for narrow to wide wedges (1 is narrow wedge and 5 is wide). As you descend, count from 1 to 5 slowly and change your A shape to match the number. Test yourself by calling the numbers out of order and assuming each wedge shape.

HEADLIGHTS. Treat your knees as headlights and point them down the hill. This helps to prevent the skis from crossing.

THROUGH THE GATE. Plant your ski poles halfway down the hill with enough room for you to ski between them. Ski to the poles in a wedge and change to a parallel position to move through the "gate." Change back to a wedge to control your building speed.

BUMPS AND DIPS. Find a section of trail with bumps and dips. Ski in a wedge across this uneven terrain and let your legs bend and extend independently of each other to handle it. Vary the shape of the wedge to control or build your speed as you wish.

Problem	Solution
Hinging	Raise the torso to prevent bending at the waist. Use the Chair Sitting and Sightseeing exercises to remain upright and centered over the skis.
Crossed tips	Flatten the skis to avoid overedging and point your knees down the hill, as in Headlights. Steering the skis farther apart into a wider wedge also helps.
Knock knees	Move the knees apart to avoid extreme edging. Review the Basic Stance and hold an imaginary basketball between your knees while you ski.
Railing	Too much weight is over the ski that is "railed" (edged), and it tracks like a train on a rail. Use the Tandem Wedge exercise on flat land to redistribute weight between both skis.
Speed control	Stiff legs and a high stance promote a narrow wedge with limited speed control. Bend the legs at the ankles and knees and

brush the skis into a wider wedge. This edges the skis and controls the speed.

WEDGE TURNS (Snowplow Turns)

Once skiers are comfortable with various wedge positions, the next step is wedge turns. These turns are the most important downhill move to learn because they can greatly slow speed. All skiers at some point resort to wedge turns between other moves, often to regain their composure!

A wedge turn happens naturally from a narrower gliding wedge. The higher stance keeps the skis flatter on the snow and allows skiers to steer the skis through the turn easily. Slight directional changes are best, because skiers can change more easily from one shallow turn to the next one.

If you find yourself locked into a braking wedge and unable to turn, you are probably struggling to slow your speed. I've watched people push themselves to handle a hill that's too challenging for their abilities. Find a gentler hill that lets you use a narrower wedge and develop a feel for the steering.

Skiers steer their skis in the direction of the turn by rotating their feet and legs. But remembering a basic wedge position is important, because they must return to this neutral stance in order to change their direction. Too often, skiers rush their turns and forget to pause for this important intermediate step.

Simply looking in the direction of the turn or pointing in that direction may be effective in initiating a turn. It appears to happen magically, but the legs are really steering the skis through the turn. Gradually, skiers add more edging and weight transfer to shape the turns.

A good goal is the performance of smoothly linked turns despite changes in terrain. A rhythmic rising and settling of the body helps to promote flowing turns. Skiers are wise to practice one turn at a time initially before attempting linked turns. One turn may be weaker than

A *wedge turn* requires an active steering of the skis in the direction of the turn. Steering the ski begins with the foot and involves a rotation of the entire leg.

the other, and on a wide hill you can keep turning in this direction with a series of turns.

Skiers can also strengthen the weaker side by beginning a series of linked turns with a turn to the poor side. That strategy promotes good practice before speed builds excessively on the hill. Skiing without poles may be helpful initially, but eventually skiers hold their poles with the hands low and in front of the body.

Practice

Skills: Sliding, steering, skidding, edging, moving from ski to ski.

Terrain: Flat.

BIG TOE TURNS. Stand with the skis parallel and a pole planted between the tips. Lift one ski and press the tip against the pole. Feel how your big toe presses against the boot. This motion simulates the steering that occurs when turning a ski. The big toe points in the direction of the turn and presses against the boot.

The other foot also needs to steer in the direction of the turn. Plant the pole to the outside of the other foot and press the outside of the foot against the pole. Press the big toe toward the pole and feel the pressure of the outside of the ski against the pole.

Ski downhill, execute a gliding wedge, and press both big toes in the direction you want to go.

KNEES PLEASE. Repeat the Big Toe exercise, but press the knee toward the ski pole and feel the added pressure against the pole. Steering the knees as well as the feet in the direction of the turn helps to create a stronger turn. Ski downhill in a gliding wedge and let your knees follow your toes in steering through the turn.

When linking turns, your toes point straight down the fall line between turns.

SCUFFING. As you begin the turn, scuff the snow a little harder under the ball of your outside foot. (If you squash with the right foot, you'll turn left.) It's as if the foot is scuffing away bubble gum or squashing a bug. This adds a little extra pressure to the turn by transferring weight to the outside ski.

TANDEM TURNS. This flatland drill is an excellent one for people who are having difficulty with the speed of hills and control of their turns. One person stands on the skis in the basic wedge position. Without skis, the partner stands behind the skier and pushes him or her across the snow. The skier steers one way by rotating the feet and then steers the other way. Gradually the partner can push harder and faster to simulate hill conditions that require the skier to steer more strongly.

HEADLIGHTS. Think of your knees as headlights that shine on the path you are skiing. The knees point straight along the curved path to light the way. Don't let the headlights cross (knees in a knock-kneed position) or the skis may cross also.

GOOD POSTURE. Hold your poles in front of you, like a tray, and adopt a properly upright torso position. Let the tray lead the way through the turns.

LANDMARKS. Use land features along the hill or numbers on the face of the clock to help the turning. Steer your knees and feet toward a landmark midway down the hill or toward three o'clock. Think of the fall line as twelve o'clock and the turns occurring toward three o'clock.

ANKLE FLEXES. Focus on bending your ankles through the turns. The ankles straighten to initiate a turn and bend through the turn. Press your shin against the tongue of the boot for good ankle bend. Keep the ankles relaxed for smooth transitions.

TALLER, SMALLER. Bend your ankles and knees to be smaller through the turn and then stand taller on the skis to initiate the next turn. Standing taller flattens the skis and lets them slide more easily into a neutral position and gliding wedge in preparation for the next turn.

POINT A TO B. Pick two points along a hill and use easy linked turns on the descent. Then ski the same course and try to execute more turns. In subsequent runs, steer harder through the turns to keep increasing the number of turns.

WEDGE REBOUNDS. Try this exercise on a gentle hill. From a parallel stance down the fall line, step into a wedge stance as you ski downhill. Then step with the other leg into a wedge. Step more quickly from wedge to wedge and rebound rhythmically from the outside ski.

TRAVERSES. Ski across the hill on a diagonal line in a traverse position, skis parallel and each ski under the shoulder. This wide stance offers good stability. Use wedge turns to round the corner and traverses between them.

SLALOM COURSES. Begin with a course where the poles appear in a straight line and require shallow directional changes. Then graduate to an offset course where the poles are farther apart. This course requires rounder turns with greater directional changes.

Begin to anticipate the next turn by rotating your torso in that direction, before your legs begin to steer. These independent actions of the upper and lower body set the stage for more advanced downhill moves.

Problem	**Solution**
Refer to Wedge problems in previous section.	
Overactive upper body	Excessive rotation of the shoulders through the turn means the legs are not performing

their job properly. Return to the Big Toe, Knees Please, and Headlight exercises to emphasize steering by the feet and knees. Keep the torso relatively quiet.

SKATE TURN

Skiers who can execute wedge turns have experimented with building and dampening their speed, and they are usually ready for the skate turn. The skate turn is a way to change directions without losing speed. In fact, it increases momentum and enables skiers to turn aggressively around a corner.

The skis diverge in a skate turn, unlike a wedge turn where the skis converge. (Crossed tips can be a problem in the wedge, but runaway skis are more often the problem with a skate turn!) The V shape lets skiers rock off their ski edges to glide around the corner. The skate turn requires good balance on each gliding ski to ride out the increasing speed.

A skier glides diagonally across a hill, steps off the uphill ski onto the downhill or inside ski that is angled in the new direction. The skier edges the uphill ski and provides a strong platform from which to push off. The pushing off propels the skier's body over the new gliding ski, and the skis are matched side by side to continue skating around the corner.

A step turn—the turn of a thousand steps—is a good introduction to the skate turn. Skiers simply take many small steps around a corner and ride out the momentum. A little edging prevents washing out or skidding, but the turn is generally a passive one. It requires an active transfer of weight from ski to ski, however, and it is an important developmental step for skiers who have difficulty gliding on one ski. Stay with small steps until one-ski balance improves.

The skate turn can evolve naturally from the step turn if skiers begin to take slightly larger steps. As they step diagonally forward, they'll edge their skis securely and develop a feel for the degree to which they can push off. The poles can be used to push onto the new gliding ski. As

A skier transfers weight quickly from ski to ski as he steps around a corner in a *skate turn.*

skiers develop confidence, they double-pole with each skate around the corner to provide additional speed.

The skate turn is most exhilarating, and I love to challenge myself by choosing increasingly sharp corners to skate around or by doing quick turns down the fall line until the speed forces me to change strategies.

Practice

Skills: Sliding, gliding on one ski, moving from ski to ski, edging, pushing, poling.

Terrain: Flat to gentle hill.

BASIC STANCE. Review the basic position practiced in the no-pole skating exercises. Step sideways in a V, tails together and tips apart. Keep bringing the skis parallel as you step. This closed position with legs together keeps you balanced and centered over the skis, ready to step sideways and push off the other ski securely without skidding out.

Take tiny steps at first and gradually take larger steps. Watch how the ski edges more as you step farther away from it.

STAR TURNS. Plant a ski pole behind your ski tails. Step around the pole by opening the tips into the V shape and keeping the tails near the pole. Take small steps, then bigger ones. Begin slowly, then increase the tempo so you are stepping faster and faster around the pole. Increased edging occurs naturally as you push off the outside ski. Practice changing directions. Then hop from ski to ski as you turn around the pole.

AT THE CORNER. Plant a marker such as a ski pole in an open expanse of snow. Double-pole across flat terrain or a gentle downhill slope toward the pole and use a skate turn to round the corner. A looping turn usually results at first, but eventually try to turn tighter around the pole. Practice turning in both directions. This exercise is a good transition to skate turns on a trail, where you have more obstacles to avoid and are forced to follow the trail.

TORSO SWIVELS. As you skate from ski to ski, the torso should face the ski tip of the leading ski. Project your torso forward into each turn to keep the body moving with the skis.

FIGURE EIGHTS. Skate in a figure-eight pattern across the snow. No-pole skating down the straightaways helps to build momentum for using skate turns on the corners. Add double poling around the corner when it feels comfortable to increase your speed.

FLATLAND SLALOM. Use a straight-line slalom course first, which requires shallow skate turns around the poles. For a greater challenge, use an offset course where more aggressive turns are needed to turn sharply around the poles.

SKATE ZIGZAGS. Skate across a hill, pushing off the downhill ski to get good glide on the ski heading slightly up the hill. Use a skate turn to round the corner and continue skating across the hill. Now you'll be practicing a strong push-off from the new downhill ski.

Problem	Solution
Poor balance	An ability to balance on a quickly gliding ski is necessary. Take smaller steps around the corner and return to flatter terrain. The one-ski exercises in Chapter 3 are also helpful.
Weak push-off	Being centered over the outside ski is important to push off diagonally forward. The Torso Swivel exercise helps to keep the body aligned over the leading ski as it steps around the corner. Again, practice exercises for gliding on one ski are valuable.

CHRISTIES

Once skiers perform smoothly linked wedge turns, they are ready for the practice of christies. A christy is a skidded turn in which both skis are skidding on corresponding edges at some point in the turn. Christies evolve naturally from a wedge with angled skis to a skidded parallel stance.

This transition signals a significant change for some skiers, because it requires more commitment than earlier moves do. Christies require an

A *stem christy turn* begins with a wedge before the skier skids his skis into a parallel stance to finish the turn.

edge change to leave the wedge position; you flatten the inside ski and slide it into position next to the outside ski during the turn. You must transfer weight to the outside ski in order to unweight the inside ski and move it across the snow. Each leg is steered independently in the same direction through the turn.

Using a narrow gliding wedge is helpful. Standing up tall as you move the skis into the wedge position flattens the skis. It allows you to steer the flattened inside ski into the parallel position. As you steer through the fall line, sink lower on the skis and prepare to stand up during the next one.

Christies usually develop easily by matching the skis in the parallel stance and skidding near *the end* of the turn. A moderate hill then offers an opportunity to turn more quickly and skid the skis on corresponding edges earlier in the turn. On steeper hills, skiers should be matching their skis when or before they steer them through the fall line.

A common problem for skiers is finding the wedge position too comfortable to give up. Sideslipping exercises can help you to become comfortable with lateral (sideways) and downhill skidding of the skis. Practice these exercises separately from christies to develop comfort with skidding. Early practice of sideslipping then enables you to execute christy turns and concentrate on the independent steering that is required of each leg.

I like the stability of the wedge christy in variable snow conditions because it offers excellent side-to-side stability (unlike the telemark turn). It also lets me control my speed at the beginning of the turn, which can be reassuring on narrower trails.

Practice

Skills: Sliding, gliding on one leg, moving from ski to ski, steering, skidding, edging, poling.

Terrain: Gentle to moderate hills.

BASIC STANCE. Practice the sequence in place to feel the up-and-down action of the body. Stand tall and slide one ski into position for a narrow gliding wedge. Step on this outside ski and bring the other ski parallel to it in a wide stance. Sink lower. Then stand tall and repeat the same steps on the other side. As you stem the ski, it becomes your new outside ski. Practice the sequence until the straightening and bending of your legs feels rhythmic.

WEDGE-CHRISTY GARLANDS. Perform continuous wedge turns in a garland across a hill, turning in only one direction from a traverse. Then repeat the sequence in the same direction and steer the inside leg actively so that it matches the other ski at the end and christy turns result. Stand tall, in a wedge, steer the skis through the turn and sink to finish the turn.

Try it in the other direction. Strive for a smooth rising and sinking.

MINI GARLANDS. Perform two garlands of christies in one direction, then turn with a wedge and do two christy garlands in the new direction. Use the sequence of double christies until the skidding feels smooth. Then change to linked christy turns (one turn in each direction).

LIFT-OFF. Traverse across a hill, steer around the corner with a wedge, and raise your body as if it is a plane lifting off. Slide the skis together and skid through the end of the turn. Let your arms aid in the raising of your body by lifting these "wings" gently.

INHALE-EXHALE. Begin the turn with a wedge and inhale deeply as you raise your body. Slide your skis parallel and exhale as you settle into the traverse.

SKI LIFTS. Begin the turn with a wedge, transfer your weight to the outside ski, and lift the inside ski off the ground and into a parallel position next to the other ski. Gradually lift the ski only a little so that the ski slides gently across the snow.

TALLER, SMALLER. During the wedge, drop lower to get smaller, then spring upward through the turn to get taller. Match the inside ski to the outside one when taller in the turn. Go smaller again to finish skidding the turn.

STOMP TURNS. During the wedge, push off the inside ski strongly, stand on the outside ski, and match the inside ski to the other one.

LIGHTEN UP. As you slide into wedge, "lighten up" the inside ski. As you steer through the fall line, let the light inside ski drift into place next to the outside ski. This forces the outside ski to do most of the turning. Try lightening the inside ski to a point where you lift it from the snow!

POLE-PLANTS. Plant the pole gently as you initiate the turn. Use a "touch-turn" rhythm for the timing. As you introduce more up-and-down body action, use the poling to help you initiate the rising of the body to begin the turn. Use a "touch-and-up" rhythm for good timing.

SLALOM COURSE. Use christy turns in a straight-line course to develop shorter, narrower turns, and offset slalom courses for rounder, longer turns. A mix of poles in different sequences—straight line and offset—encourages the practice of different types of christies.

Terrain: Steep hill.

SIDESLIPPING. Stand sideways across the fall line with the skis edged against the hill. The knees and ankles roll into the hill to edge the skis. Flatten them by rolling the knees and ankles down the hill, to begin the sideslip. Stop the sideslipping by edging again and sinking down. Vary the edging to experiment with quick and gradual stopping. The emphasis here is edge control.

TIP SLIDES. Stand sideways across the fall line and steer the ski tips downhill. Let the skis slide at this angle before you steer the tips across the hill again and edge the skis to stop skidding. Although the skis may feel more comfortable in a wedge as you turn through the fall line, strive to keep them parallel as much as possible. The emphasis is steering control.

ONE-SKI SIDESLIPPING. Stand on one ski across the fall line and practice sideslipping with the downhill leg first. Then wear the ski on the uphill leg for sideslipping. Exercise both legs equally and strengthen the ability to sideslip on inside and outside edges of the skis. This exercise develops independent leg action.

ONE-SKI GARLANDS. Perform continuous christies in a garland across a hill, skiing on the "downhill" ski. Push off with the free "uphill" foot to descend the hill slightly and then turn uphill.

SIDESLIP SPINS. Sideslip downhill, then steer the tips around the corner and sideslip facing in the opposite direction. You'll end up spinning 180 degrees.

POINT A TO B. Keep sideslipping and turning between two points. Ski the course again and try to turn more times.

HOCKEY STOPS. Stop skidding at the end of a christy by edging sharply and checking your speed.

Problem	Solution
Edge changes	An inability to move the inside ski from the wedge to a parallel position is caused by too much weight and edging on the inside ski. Using the Lift-Off, Inhale-Exhale, and One-Ski Lift exercises helps to raise the body, flatten the ski, and transfer weight to the outside ski. Make sure you begin from a narrow gliding wedge.

Excessive skidding	More edging is needed to control the turn. Use the Sideslipping exercises and vary the degree of edging.

PARALLEL TURN

A parallel turn keeps the skis equidistant or parallel from beginning to end, and it evolves naturally from the christy. As skiers begin to skid their skis earlier in a christy, they move toward a parallel turn. The goal is initiating the parallel turn without a wedge.

A beginning parallel turn uses a wide stance with the skis under the hips to improve balance. Practice on a well-groomed slope where few bumps can disrupt your rhythm. The skis may skid through the turn at the outset, but as skiers improve they strive to carve the turn by edging their skis more strongly.

Development of strong steering with both skis began with the christy and continues here to improve the parallel turn. A skier who stands tall to initiate the turn can shift weight to the outside ski and steer both skis through the turn. Once skiers graduate to more difficult terrain, the need to steer each ski independently will increase.

More exaggerated up-and-down movement with the body makes a parallel turn more dynamic. This bending and extending involves the *ankles* and the knees. Skiers extend their legs and lighten the skis to steer them through the turn. Then they sink again at the end to finish and control the turn.

They also begin to project their bodies down the fall line, reaching down to plant their poles. This aggressive action keeps their momentum traveling down the hill rather than back into the hill. It involves an increasing separation of the upper and lower body as terrain steepens. Twisting or rotating the torso away from the legs (and facing downhill) during the turn sets the skier up for the next turn. The upper body has already anticipated the new turn and helps to move the legs in the new direction.

An extension of the legs during a *parallel turn* lifts the skis and helps to steer them in the direction of the turn.

When I first struggled with parallel turns on steep terrain, I wasn't willing to anticipate the next turn and face it fully with my torso. I tended to "back away" from the turn with the result that when I fell it was inevitably back into the hill. Better than falling downhill on my head, I thought! But when I finally risked projecting my torso down the hill into the next turn, the turns worked magically.

Practice

Skills: Sliding, gliding on one ski, moving from ski to ski, steering, skidding, edging, poling.

Terrain: Moderate to steep hills.

BASIC STANCE. Without skis, use poles for balance and stand flat-footed on the snow. Swivel your feet by pointing your big toes in one direction and then the opposite way. Increase the swiveling by letting your knees point with your feet. A rhythmic up-and-down flow occurs naturally. Finish the practice by separating your upper body from your legs; rotate the torso away from the legs.

HOPS. Swivel your skis in place by hopping gently and rotating your feet. Let the skis slide gently across the snow as you mark an X in the snow with your skis. The legs bend and straighten naturally to hop up and down.

PARALLEL GARLANDS. Ski down a hill on a diagonal and steer your tips uphill slightly. Steer in that direction with both big toes and perform several shallow turns. (Your weight remains distributed along the entire foot. Just press the toes in the direction of the turn.) Now add additional steering with your knees.

To ease any struggle with the turns, extend your legs to help steer the skis, and bend them to come to a stop.

ONE-LEGGED PARALLEL GARLANDS. Repeat the previous exercise and begin the turns by steering both skis. But shift weight to your downhill or outside ski and lighten the inside ski.

CHRISTIES TO PARALLELS. Begin with christy turns, emphasizing the step onto the outside ski. Gradually eliminate the initial wedge and simply step onto the outside ski and begin to steer it into the fall line. At the same time, lighten the inside ski and steer it in the parallel position to follow the other ski.

BUMP SWIVELS. Stand on top of a bump so your tips and tails are free of the snow. Swivel or rotate your legs and skis from side to side as if you are linking turns. Rotate your upper body and arms in the opposite direction. The skis stay flat through the swiveling and may edge a bit at the end.

Then ski toward a bump, or "mogul," plant your pole on it and turn around on top of it. As you approach the fall line, your legs are swiveled one way and your torso is rotated the other way. The torso leans down the hill and "looks" for the next bump to turn around.

This exercise requires an open slope with gentler bumps.

TOUCH-AND-UP. Time the pole-plants so they initiate the turns. Touch the pole to the inside of the turn and raise the body to turn. Touching the snow gently tends to create a smooth, flowing rhythm. Then change the touch to a quick jab so the skiing tempo quickens.

The free outside hand should come forward as you plant the pole. This helps to keep your torso forward, moving toward the next turn.

ANKLES UP. Increase your ability to absorb changes in terrain by focusing on more ankle bend. This flexion lets you spring up more dynamically as you turn. Bend the ankles more to sink lower through the fall line.

KNEES PLEASE. Link parallel turns and steer through the turn with your knees to get extra oomph. The inside knee is especially important, and it can help to make quicker, sharper turns.

PLATFORMS. Stand sideways across the hill. Jump up and down on your skis, edging them as you land to create a stable platform. Experiment with how aggressive you can be and still maintain your balance. Plant the downhill pole to provide more support.

Link turns down the fall line, and use these platforms to check the speed of your turn or to launch your next move. The downhill pole can be planted when you land and sink or when you spring to help begin the new move.

WEDGE HOPPERS. Start downhill in a wedge position and shift weight to one ski. Spring off this ski and land on the other ski. Hop back and forth from one angled ski to the other, letting your legs move from side to side while your torso remains centered. Use your poles near the tips as needed for balance.

PARASKATES. Skate across a moderate hill, skate onto the uphill ski, and use a parallel turn to round the corner. Skate across the hill in the new direction and use a parallel turn again on the corner.

Problem	Solution
Refer to the previous section on Christies.	
Excessive skidding	More edging is needed to shape the turns and move toward carving them. Use the Platforms exercise for aggressive edging.

TELEMARK

The telemark turn is an elegant, powerful turn that provides stability under a variety of conditions. The skier dips into the bent-knee stance of the telemark, and the two skis form a curved arc like a single long ski. This position lowers the center of gravity and increases a skier's stability from front to back. It's especially useful when skiing with a pack, because the skier simply lifts a heel off one ski and sinks forward into the "curtsy" of the telemark.

The telemark turn has many variations, but they have one common ingredient: the basic telemark position. It's important to develop an effi-

A skier can use a half-wedge position to begin the *telemark turn* before sinking into the telemark position.

cient stance at the beginning, because successful turns cannot happen without it. This developmental stage is often rushed by skiers who want to move quickly to turns, but they suffer frustration with problems that are often traced to a glitch in the basic pose.

The telemark attracts both alpine and Nordic skiers who want a new challenge in downhill skiing. Alpine skiers may feel more comfortable with high-speed telemark turns, while Nordic skiers may be more at ease with the sensation of balancing on free-heeled equipment. These exercises draw on skills from both skiing worlds because the dynamics are the same.

The basic telemark position can be modified depending upon snow conditions, terrain, and personal style. Some skiers can adopt a higher stance that lets them change strategies quickly, and others go for a low position that increases stability. The versatile telemark skier is one who can switch smoothly from one to the other, reacting to changes in terrain. The staggered foot placement of the telemark does tend to lessen a skier's stability side to side, which is no problem for the skier who can change effortlessly to parallel turns. Alternating between both turns is great advanced practice!

A step telemark in which the skis are stemmed initially to slow the skier is effective on steep terrain. Skiers can almost walk down steep hills in these "braking" telemarks. Jump telemarks are great for leaping around moguls or leaping free of crusty snow. Some of my best days on telemark skis have been shared with an enthusiastic group of friends—using trees as slalom poles, then swooping out onto open slopes, exploring little-known trails in New England.

Practice

Skills: Sliding, gliding on one ski, moving from ski to ski, steering, skidding, edging, poling.

Terrain: Flat.

BASIC STANCE. Stand with skis parallel, slide one ski forward, and sink down onto it until the heel lifts off the other ski. The torso is straight, with the shoulder and hip directly above the knee of the trailing ski. The knee of the trailing ski drops straight down toward the heel of the leading foot.

Weight is equally distributed between the two skis. The legs should be close together for a tighter stance rather than spread apart (when looking from the front).

Practice this position, giving each leg an opportunity to be the leading leg. Sink into a position that feels comfortable for your skeletal structure. Some skiers prefer a higher stance, while others like a lower stance.

CHANGE-UPS. Sink into the telemark position, then rise until the feet are side by side, and sink on the other side. Close your eyes and drop into the position again. Check your position to make sure the trailing knee is under the hips and shoulders.

POP-UPS. Pop up and down from one telemark position to the other with a smooth transition. The skis slide back and forth on the snow as a bouncy rhythm develops. Holding the poles at their midlengths helps keep them out of the way and the hands low and near the thighs.

STRIDING. Stride across the snow and sink into the telemark position with every third stride. Use your poles naturally to stride and then tuck them behind you when you drop into the position. The hands stay low and near the thighs.

Terrain: Gentle hill.

TELLY TRAVERSES. Double-pole across a hill and sink into the telemark position with the downhill ski leading. Don't try to turn into the hill at first. The torso faces downhill slightly and offsets the legs angled into the hill to edge the skis.

On a wide hill, keep double poling and sinking into the telemark position. Use a wedge turn around the corner and practice the telemark position with the new downhill ski leading.

Repeat the sequence with a new twist. Sink into the telemark position and steer the downhill foot and knee into the hill. A brief uphill turn should result. Keep practicing these uphill turns while zigzagging down the hill.

STRAIGHT RUN TELLIES. Ski down the fall line and alternate the telemark positions. Sink rhythmically, and when necessary, stay in the straight run to regain balance.

Then walk or stride down, sliding the leading ski forward smoothly and sinking into position with each step.

Descend the hill, drop into the telemark position, and steer gently with the foot and knee. Rise to an upright position, drop into the other telemark position, and then steer.

The result is gentle, shallow turns. Don't rush them. Sink into the basic position first, then steer. Your weight should be distributed equally between your skis.

HALF-WEDGE STRAIGHT RUN. Ski down the fall line and brush out one ski into a half-wedge position. Keep the straight ski flat on the snow. Then return to the straight run position and brush out the other ski. Use a narrow half wedge to avoid setting the straight ski on edge.

Shift a little weight to the outside ski to begin half-wedge turns. Still keep more weight on the flat inside ski through the turns.

The straight ski will become the trailing (inside) ski in a telemark turn. Keeping weight on it in this exercise eliminates a potential problem with transferring too much weight to the leading ski. It also flattens the soon-to-be-trailing ski so that it can skid next to the leading ski in the telemark position.

HALF-WEDGE TELLIES. Use a half wedge to initiate the turn and sink into the telemark position when coming through the fall line. Let the heel lift off the trailing (inside) ski, and slide the trailing ski closer to the leading (outside) ski to align them. Steer both skis through the turn.

Gradually sink into the telemark position earlier in the turn so that steering in the telemark happens before the fall line. Rising up slightly can help the transition from the half wedge to the telemark when the trailing ski slides next to the leading ski. A pole-plant can also help to raise the body.

Eventually, practice linked telemark turns from the half-wedge position, keeping the turns shallow with little directional change.

SKATING TELLIES. Skate across a hill, skate onto the uphill ski, and sink into a telemark turn to round the corner. (The uphill skating ski becomes the leading ski.) Keep skating across the hill in the new direction and skate onto the uphill ski before dropping into the telemark. Once in the position, distribute your weight between the two skis.

Repeat the sequence, but skate onto the downhill ski and then drop into the telemark. (The downhill skating ski becomes the trailing ski.) Again, distribute your weight between the two skis.

These exercises ask skiers to balance completely over one ski at first, before they sink into the telemark position where they weight both skis. The independent action of each leg is strengthened.

STEP TELEMARKS. Step the uphill (outside) ski into a half-wedge position, transferring more than half your weight onto the ski. Slide the trailing ski near the leading ski as you sink into the telemark position.

Then rise and step the other outside ski into a half-wedge position to repeat the sequence on the other side. The step telemark makes you step around and across the fall line to break your speed. The move controls momentum on very steep terrain.

Terrain may interfere with sliding the trailing ski into position. If so, lift it and move it into position next to the leading ski. You've completely transferred your weight to the outside ski. The move becomes a two-step telemark as you move each ski into position in a staggered or sequential fashion.

LEG PUMPS. Traverse across a hill and "pump" the uphill (trailing) ski several times. It develops a bouncy up-and-down rhythm. To turn the corner, pump one last time on the uphill leg, slide it forward into the telemark position, and weight it. Both skis steer around the corner.

The exercise completely weights the trailing leg momentarily, before the weight is equally distributed between the skis. It's helpful to the skier who fails to weight the rear ski.

LEG LIFTS. Lift the outside (leading) ski and slide it forward into the telemark position to steer through the turn. This exercise also weights the rear leg momentarily to prevent it from skidding out.

TOE TURNS. As you steer through the turn, press the big toe of your leading foot against the boot into the turn. The little toe of the trailing foot should also press against the boot. This strengthens steering and edging.

JUMP TELLIES. These springy telemark turns are more of a simultaneous action than step telemarks. In a stationary position, sink low into a telemark and spring up, twisting your skis in the opposite direction before you land in the new telemark position. The leading ski changes in the air.

On the hill, begin in a telemark position across the fall line, spring into the air, and twist around to face in the opposite direction across the fall line. Again, the leading ski changes in the air. Jump tellies are a good way to negotiate moguls and wet or crusty snow.

A double pole-plant can help you to spring up into the new position. A single pole-plant also works. Keep the pole-plant from the previous turn in the snow until you plant the new pole and jump into the air.

POINT A TO B. Perform telemark turns between two points and count the number of turns. Ski the course again and try to do as many telemarks as possible. The best choice is step or jump telemarks to keep braking down the hill.

TORSO ROTATION. Twist your torso away from the direction in which your legs are turning. This separates the upper body from the lower body and helps to keep it oriented down the hill in anticipation of the next turn.

GLOVE TURNS. Hold a glove between your thighs and execute short turns down the fall line. This is a fun exercise to test whether your legs stay close together and align the two skis almost as one ski through the turn.

MONOMARK. Use one telemark position and turn in both directions from this stance. Carve the turns by changing your edges. A challenging task!

TANDEM TELEMARKS. Hold hands with a partner and perform synchronized telemark turns. A partnership provides stability through the turns with side-to-side support, but be ready to let go if falling is inevitable.

FUNNELS. Begin with wide, gradual turns and gradually shorten them until you finish with short, quick turns. The change creates a funnel path down the hill and forces you to make increasingly aggressive moves down the fall line.

Problem	Solution
Unweighted rear leg	Distribute weight equally between the leading and trailing leg. Return to the Basic Stance, stand completely on one ski, and slide the other ski forward to sink into the telemark position. Use the Half-Wedge ex-

ercises with their emphasis on a flat, weighted inside ski.

Crossing tails	Again, the inside trailing ski needs to be weighted and steered through the turn. Use Leg Pumps and Leg Lifts to momentarily weight the inside ski before sliding the leading ski into position.
Skidding out	Eliminate overrotation caused by excessive shoulder swing. Use the Torso Rotation exercise to orient the upper body down the fall line. Also reach down the hill for your next pole-plant to keep your torso moving away from the hill rather than into it.
Stemming	Flatten the inside ski to move from a wedge position where the ski is edged against the snow. Use the Half-Wedge Straight Run to emphasize a flat trailing ski and a narrow wedge.

Glossary

All-Purpose Sports Stance. A neutral, balanced stance from which a skier executes all moves; the upper body is upright, the legs and ankles are flexed, and the hands remain in front of the body.

Angulation. The bending of the body along its central axis that allows the legs and torso to lean in different directions.

Alpine Skiing. A discipline that primarily involves downhill-skiing techniques; the equipment affixes the entire foot to the ski.

Christy. A skidded turn in which the skis are parallel and skid on the same edges at some point in the turn.

Counter-Rotation. A difference in pivoting actions between the torso and the legs. The torso turns one way and the legs turn the opposite way.

Cross-Country Downhill Skiing. A blend of alpine and Nordic skiing moves also known as "telemarking." The equipment blends metal-edged skis with a three-pin binding.

Diagonal V. A skating maneuver to glide aggressively uphill with the skis in a V-shaped position, tips apart and tails together.

Diagonal Stride. The most common cross-country maneuver for gliding across flat terrain and up hills. The term refers to the alternating action of arms and legs similar to that found in walking.

Double Poling. A maneuver in which both arms push on the poles simultaneously to provide forward momentum. The upper body follows the arms to provide extra energy.

Edging. A skill in which the bottom corner of a ski digs into the snow. The greater the tilt of the ski, the greater the edging.

Fall Line. The imaginary line that follows the greatest angle of the slope.

Free-Glide Side. The ski over which no poling occurs in skating moves.

Garland. A pattern of turns across a hill that resembles a garland on a Christmas tree. The turns are consecutive and in the same direction.

Gliding Herringbone. A maneuver to slide uphill with skis in a V-shaped position, tips apart and tails together.

Gliding On One Ski. One of the most essential skiing skills; the skier is centered over one ski.

Herringbone. A maneuver to step uphill with the skis in a V-shaped position. A half herringbone uses a modified or half-V position.

Kick Double Pole. Double poling combined with an extra push from the leg; also known as a single-step double pole. The swing of the leg provides more power than double poling alone.

Maneuver. A combination of skills that create a more complex movement on snow.

Marathon Skate. Double poling combined with an extra push from an angled,or skating, ski. The technique is used in ski tracks to gain extra power.

Moving from Ski to Ski. A skill that involves the transfer of weight from one ski to the other one. Complete weight transfer occurs when the skier is centered over one ski at a time.

Nordic Skiing. A discipline that involves cross-country and downhill maneuvers. The equipment affixes the toe to the ski and leaves the heel free.

Parallel Turn. A turning technique in which the skis remain in a parallel, or side-by-side, stance from beginning to end.

Poling. A skill where a planting of the poles increases a skier's momentum or guides a skier through a turn; a timing device that aids rhythmic skiing.

Power Side. The ski over which the poling occurs in skating moves.

Pushing Off. A skill that creates good traction and propels a skier forward; also known as "gripping" because the ski's wax pocket grips the snow to create traction; also known as the "kick."

Sideslipping. A skidding of the skis to the side and forward down the hill.

Sidestepping. Moving sideways by lifting one ski at a time across the snow.

Single Step Double Pole. A technique that combines double poling with an extra push from the leg; also known as a kick double pole. The swing of the leg provides more power than does double poling alone.

Skate Turn. A turning technique with which a skier can accelerate around corners with the skis in a V-shaped position. The skier steps off one ski, steps onto the diverging ski, and brings the other ski parallel.

Skating (no poles). A maneuver to provide forward momentum where the skis form a V or angled shape. The skier steps off one ski, glides onto the diverging ski and then glides back to the original ski.

Skidding. A skill in which the skis slip sideways or around against the snow.

Skill. A simple action or task that is part of a more complex move; proficiency in performing a task.

Steering. A skill where the rotary force of the leg and foot turns the ski.

Straight Run. A maneuver where the skier slides downhill in a relaxed, centered stance. The skis are parallel.

Telemark Turn. The oldest turning maneuver; the skier sinks into a "curtsy" and the skis form one long curve to carve a stable turn.

V1. A skating maneuver that combines double poling with skating. The skier poles only once for every two skating steps. The move is used on groomed snow with no tracks.

V2. A fast skating technique that combines double poling with skating. The skier poles twice for every two skating steps. The move is used on groomed snow with no tracks.

V2 Alternate. A skating technique similar to V2 except poling occurs only once for every two skating steps. Skating and poling are not synchronized as in V1.

Wedge. A fundamental downhill maneuver to control speed. The skier angles the skis inward in an "A" shape and presses them against the snow; also known as the snowplow. A braking wedge is wider, with the skis edged more aggressively against the snow. A gliding wedge is narrower, with the skis flatter to the snow.

Wedge Turns. A turning maneuver with the skis in an A-shaped position. Linked wedge turns are usually gliding wedges, where the narrower width makes it easier to begin and end the turn.

Index